DENISE SAMSON

PONCHOS
to knit

More than 40 Projects and Paired Accessories in Classic and Contemporary Styles

TRAFALGAR SQUARE
North Pomfret, Vermont

First published in the United States of America
in 2017 by
Trafalgar Square Books
North Pomfret, Vermont 05053

Originally published in Norwegian as *Poncho*.

ISBN: 978-1-57076-824-8

Library of Congress Control Number: 2017934552

Book Design: Laila Sundet Gundersen
Cover Design: RM Didier
Head Photographer: Guri Pfeifer Photo
Photographs (pages 20-23, 29-31, and 51-52): Anita
Hamremoen
Charts: Denise Samson
Technical Consultant: May Britt Bjella Zamori
Translator: Carol Huebscher Rhoades

Printed in China

10 9 8 7 6 5 4 3 2 1

CONTENTS

5 ...... Preface and Acknowledgments
6 ...... Various Poncho Silhouettes
7 ...... Abbreviations
8 ...... Oman Poncho
11 ...... Headband
12 ...... Twisted Stitch Sweater-Poncho
14 ...... Wrist Warmers
16 ...... Cape with Optical Illusion Cables
20 ...... Large Poncho-Sweater
23 ...... Hat and Scarf
24 ...... Pocket Scarf
26 ...... Poncho in Missoni Stripes
28 ...... Wrist Warmers
29 ...... Square Poncho
31 ...... Detached Ribbed Collar
32 ...... Classic Cabled Poncho
36 ...... Poncho with Leaf Motifs
38 ...... Wrist Warmers
40 ...... Crocheted Four-Leafed Clover Poncho
44 ...... Barcelona Poncho/Cabled Shawl
48 ...... Poncho with Short Rolled Collar
51 ...... Cable-Knit Square Poncho
54 ...... Poncho Crocheted with Blocks of Stars
58 ...... New York Skyline Poncho
62 ...... Poncho with Cables and Belt Openings
64 ...... Bell Shaped Poncho
68 ...... Honeycomb Brioche Poncho
71 ...... Net Crocheted Poncho with Picots
74 ...... Large Circular Neck/Heart Warmer
76 ...... Ribbed Poncho
78 ...... Crocheted Shawl in Lace Fan Pattern
82 ...... Poncho with Raglan Cables
86 ...... Hooded Poncho
90 ...... Short Hooded Poncho
92 ...... Crocheted Shawl in Shell Net Pattern
94 ...... Autumn Poncho
96 ...... Headband
98 ...... Celtic Knot Poncho
102 ...... Denise Poncho
106 ...... Denise Hat
108 ...... Basket-weave Cable Poncho
112 ...... Inca Pattern Poncho
114 ...... Fur Turtleneck Poncho
116 ...... Boot Toppers
118 ...... Multi-Purpose Poncho
120 ...... Poncho with Diamond Cables
122 ...... Poncho with Furry Trim
124 ...... Cowl
124 ...... Detached Cuffs
126 ...... Glittery Crocheted Shawl
129 ...... Yarn Sources

Follow me on my blog at andreboller. no, or on Facebook— search for "Andre Boller – Denise Samson."

PREFACE

The poncho—a simple but elegant garment. I always feel a little taller somehow when I'm wearing a poncho; there's something so sophisticated about them! And, happily, ponchos are back in fashion all over the world these days. Just take a look around on the bus, in shop windows, and at pictures from the fashion world's catwalks. This simple garment has become quite a craze—and not without reason! A poncho can be light or heavy, with or without fringe, neutral or patterned, an outer garment or perfect for a party. Ponchos can be made with all kinds of techniques and adjusted to suit almost any style, but they have a common denominator: they're gloriously easy to shape compared to other knitted garments.

The poncho had its peak of popularity during the 1970s, when any self-respecting hippie owned a colorful poncho. Ideally woven with water-resistant wool fabric, ponchos originated in Peru and are traditionally worn all over South America. The basic shape of the poncho is essentially a square, with an opening at the center to push the head through. Anyone who's participated in outdoor events has probably been saved from a sudden shower with a hooded rain poncho!

In this book, I've collected twenty of my own designs, most of them knitted but a few crocheted or with crocheted edges; and in addition, I've selected fifteen of my favorites from Norwegian yarn producers. I know some of the designers personally, and it was wonderful to be able to spice up the book with their designs. The names of the individual designers are included with the patterns.

Some of the designs are crosses between ponchos and sweaters, while others are more like large shawls. Most are somewhere in between, and shaped like classic ponchos. They're very straightforward to make—there's almost no finishing, other than a few easy seams.

Some of the ponchos have matching accessories like hats, headbands, wrist warmers, or boot toppers.

Oh, and one last thing: I recommend that you knit ponchos on a circular needle even when working back and forth, to make it less stressful on your shoulders, neck, and arms.

I hope this collection will inspire you to sit down and treat yourself to some cozy hours of crafting!

Denise Samson

Acknowledgments

The biggest thanks go to the publisher and my editor, Toril Blomquist, who showed faith in me and who believed that I could produce this book in record time. To the photographer, Guri Pfeifer, who once again took such fantastic photos of my work, and to Laila Sundet, who designed the interior of this lovely book. A big thank you to May Britt Bjella Zamori for one of the poncho patterns, as well as for technical editing of the manuscript. Thank you to House of Yarn, Viking of Norway, and A Knit Story for generously sharing their patterns with me. House of Yarn, Sandnes Yarn, and Tjorven also contributed yarns for my designs. A heartfelt thank you to my knitters, Anne-Grethe Kolstad, Bente Bodin Sundet, and Solbjørg Rustad, who helped me out in a pinch when I wasn't able to knit all the ponchos myself. And, of course, thank you to my dear, kind, and patient Tormod—who is equally enthusiastic about each and every one of the garments I produce. Thanks also to the models who wore these ponchos so well: Anna Pfeifer, Frøya Hetzel, Kaja Marie Lereng Kvernbakken, Linda Aagnes, and Marion Range Aasbø.

VARIOUS PONCHO SILHOUETTES

A poncho can be, in principle, something as simple as a square piece of fabric with a hole for the head. I haven't included this "ur-version" in my book, but many ponchos consist of one or two pieces with no shaping at all. A knitted or crocheted poncho will quickly conform to the body and shape itself around the shoulders and arms, even if it consists only of flat, straight pieces.

Some of the ponchos in this book were fashioned with round shaping or raglan shaping over the shoulders, but some are made of straight pieces with easy seams, which are nevertheless quite versatile. Below I've sketched some of the ways you can join a poncho—by knitting or crocheting two matching pieces that are then sewn together, or by working a single rectangular piece that can be joined at certain edges in various ways.

PONCHO SILHOUETTES

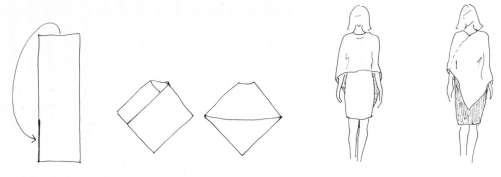

1 *A poncho made from one long, rectangular piece. One short edge is seamed to one long edge, as you can see in the sketch. The poncho has one side with a point and one side that is crossed over. It can be worn with the point to the front or the back, as desired. The Classic Cabled Poncho (page 32) and the Poncho with Leaf Motifs (page 36) are made this way.*

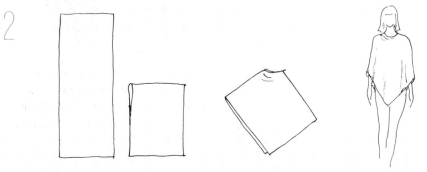

2 *This version of the poncho is made with a rectangular piece, folded double and sewn together along one side. A neck opening is formed at the top of the fold. The Poncho in Missoni Stripes (page 26) is made this way.*

3 *A poncho made from two rectangular pieces, folded double and sewn together at the sides, at the center front, and at the center back. The armholes are open at the top of the sides, and the neck opening is above the center seam. The Large Poncho-Sweater (page 20) was made this way.*

4

A poncho made from a rectangular piece folded double and sewn together, with a separate cabled piece (insert panel) at the center front (see drawing above). If desired, a hood can be added by picking up stitches around the neck. The Hooded Poncho (page 86) was made this way.

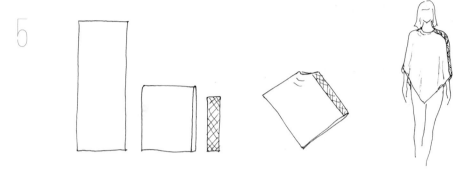

5

A poncho made from a long, rectangular piece folded double, with a separate cable panel added on the open side. In principle, this is the same as #4 above, but the poncho is turned so the point faces down and the cable cascades down one shoulder. The Celtic Knot Poncho (page 98) is made this way.

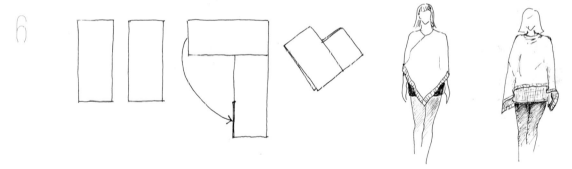

6

A poncho made from two matching, rectangular pieces, sewn together with the short side against the long side (see sketch), which makes matching points at the front and back—or, of course, it can be turned so the points are at the sides. Many of the ponchos in the book are made this way. For examples of this method, see the Square Poncho (page 29), Crocheted Four-Leafed Clover Poncho (page 40), Cable-Knit Square Poncho (page 51), Honeycomb Brioche Poncho (page 68), Net Crocheted Poncho with Picots (page 71), and Ribbed Poncho (page 76).

ABBREVIATIONS

beg	begin(s)(ning)		front and then back of same stitch
BO	bind off (= British cast off)	k2tog	knit two stitches together = 1 stitch decreased
CF	center front	k3tog	knit three stitches together = 2 stitches decreased
ch	chain		
cm	centimeter(s)	m	meter(s)
cn	cable needle	M1	make 1 = lift strand between two stitches and knit into back loop
CO	cast on		
dc	double crochet (= British treble crochet)	mm	millimeters
		p	purl
dec	decrease(s)	pm	place marker
dpn	double-pointed needles	psso	pass slipped stitch over
est	established	rem	remain(s)(ing)
inc	increase(s)	rep	repeat
k	knit	rnd(s)	round(s)
k1f&b	knit 1 front and back= knit into	RS	right side

cc	single crochet (= British double crochet)
sl	slip
slm	slip marker
ssk	(sl 1 knitwise) 2 times; knit the 2 sts together through back loops
st(s)	stitch(es)
St st	stockinette stitch (= British stocking stitch)
tog	together
tr	treble crochet (= British double treble)
WS	wrong side
wyb	with yarn held in back
wyf	with yarn held in front
yd	yard(s)
yo	yarnover

OMAN PONCHO

Design: Denise Samson

SIZES
S/M (L/XL)

FINISHED MEASUREMENTS
TOTAL LENGTH: 27½ (29½) in / 70 (75) cm
CIRCUMFERENCE, LOWER EDGE: 74 (78) in /
188 (198) cm

MATERIALS
YARN: CYCA #2 (sport/baby) Baby Silk from Du Store
Alpakka (80% baby alpaca, 20% mulberry silk; 145
yd/133 m / 50 g)
YARN AMOUNTS:
PONCHO: 500 (550) g Natural White 301, 50 (100) g Light
Blue 313
HEADBAND: Leftover yarn from poncho
NEEDLES: U.S. sizes 2.5 and 4 / 3 and 3.5 mm, circulars
24, 32, and 60 in / 60, 80, and 150 cm long for poncho;
U.S. size 4 / 3.5 mm, circular 16 in / 40 cm for headband

CROCHET HOOK: U.S. size D-3 / 3 mm
GAUGE: 24 sts in St st on larger needles = 4 in / 10 cm.
Adjust needle sizes to obtain correct gauge if necessary.

PONCHO

The idea for this poncho was taken from the
Oman sweater, which I knitted after having seen
a fantastic hooded garment for men from Oman.
I liked the sweater so much that I had to adapt it
into a poncho with the same pattern. The poncho
is knitted in the round from the top down. Change
to longer circular as necessary.

With White and shortest smaller circular, CO 108
(124) sts. Join, being careful not to twist cast-on
row; pm for beg of rnd. Work around in k2, p2
ribbing for 8¾ in / 22 cm. Change to shortest
larger circular. On the next rnd, increase 30 (32)
sts with M1 evenly spaced around = 138 (156) sts.

8

Chart 1

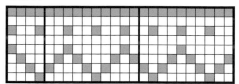

Chart 2

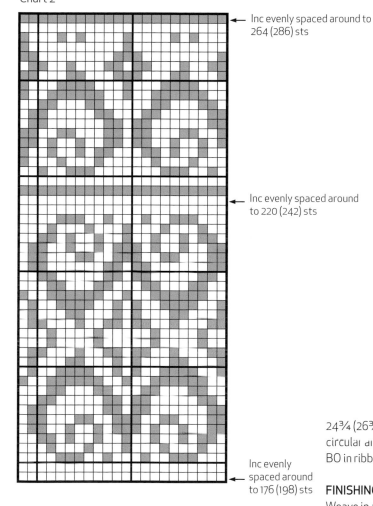

← Inc evenly spaced around to 264 (286) sts

← Inc evenly spaced around to 220 (242) sts

← Inc evenly spaced around to 176 (198) sts

Chart 3

☐ Natural White 301

▨ Light Blue 313

◿ k2tog

◎ yo

24¾ (26¾) in / 63 (68) cm. Change to smaller circular and work in k2, p2 ribbing for 2¾ in / 7 cm. BO in ribbing.

FINISHING
Weave in all ends neatly on WS. Place poncho, patted out to finished measurements, between two damp towels and leave until dry.

EDGING for Arm Openings at Sides
With White and crochet hook, work 1 rnd of single crochet around each arm opening. Work 1 rnd crab stitch (= single crochet worked from left to right).

HEADBAND

With White and 16 in / 40 cm U.S. size 4 / 3.5 mm circular, CO 110 sts. Join to knit in the rnd and pm for beg of rnd. Knit 11 rnds in St st and then work following Chart 3. After completing charted rows, knit 11 rnds in St st and BO. Sew the cast-on and bind-off rows together.

Knit 6 rnds in St st. Now work following Charts 1 and then 2 on page 11, increasing as indicated at the arrows. After completing Chart 2, knit 1 rnd and increase evenly spaced around to 316 (338) sts. Pm around 2 sts at each side. On every 4th rnd, increase 1 st at each side of the marked sts at each side. When piece measures 14½ (16½) in / 37 (42) cm, make the arm openings at each side. Divide the piece in two and work each side separately back and forth for 4¾ in / 12 cm. *At the same time*, continue to increase at the sides as established. Work the other side the same way and then join the pieces on the circular. Now increase on every 6th rnd until the piece measures

TWISTED STITCH SWEATER-PONCHO

Design: Denise Samson

SIZE
One size

FINISHED MEASUREMENTS
TOTAL LENGTH: 26 in / 66 cm
Circumference, Lower Edge:
SWEATER: 59 in / 150 cm
SLEEVELESS PONCHO: 63 in / 160 cm

MATERIALS
YARN: CYCA #3 (DK/light worsted) Sterk from Du Store Alpakka (40% Merino wool, 40% alpaca, 20% polyamide; 150 yd/137 m / 50 g)
YARN AMOUNTS:
500 g Light Gray 841
NEEDLES: U.S. size 4 / 3.5 mm, circular and set of 5 dpn; cable needle
GAUGE: 22 sts in St st = 4 in /10 cm.
Adjust needle size to obtain correct gauge if necessary.

———————————

Twisted stitches are very decorative and much simpler to make than they look. This garment is more of a sweater than a poncho, but if you prefer a sleeveless poncho and a pair of wrist warmers,

the pattern is on page 14. The pieces are knitted in the round from the bottom up.

SWEATER

CO 344 sts; join, being careful not to twist cast-on row. Pm for beg of rnd and work in pattern following Chart 1 (see page 15). Pm at each side with 172 sts between markers. Continue in St st until sweater measures 5¼ in / 13 cm. BO 6 sts at each side of marker at each side = 24 sts bound off. Set piece aside.

CUFFS

With dpn, CO 52 sts; join to work in the round. Work around in pattern following Chart 1. On the last rnd of garter st, CO 1 extra st at the center of the sleeve. Pm at center of underarm. Continue around in pattern as follows: P19, work the 15 sts of Chart 2, p19. When sleeve is 6 in / 15 cm long, BO 6 sts on each side of underarm marker = 12 sts decreased. Set piece aside and make the other cuff the same way.

RAGLAN SHAPING

Place the sleeves over the bound-off sts on each side of sweater body. Continue in pattern following Chart 2 at each side. *At the same time*, shape raglan: K2tog at the beg of the St st section, knit until 2 sts rem on the St st section, ssk. Work across sleeve sts as est and then rep the decreases on the other side = 4 sts decreased around. Dec the same way on every 4th rnd until the piece measures approx. 23¾ in / 60 cm = 266 sts rem.

SADDLE SHOULDERS

BO the first 35 sts of the St st section, work 22 sts for the neck and place these sts onto a holder, BO the next 35 sts, k41 sts for shoulder and place sts on a holder, BO the next 35 sts of St st section, work 22 sts and place those sts on a holder, BO next 35 sts. Over the last 41 sts for shoulder, work back and forth in pattern following Chart 2. Measure and BO when you have worked the same length as for the bound-off sts for front and back and up to the sts for the neck. Slip the 41 sts from the stitch holder onto needles U.S. 4 / 3.5 mm and work the other shoulder the same way.

FINISHING

Weave in all ends neatly on WS. Join underarm seams and neatly seam shoulders at front and back pieces.

NECKBAND

Beginning at one shoulder, pick up and knit 34 sts, slip the 22 sts held for back onto needle and knit, pick up and knit 34 sts along other shoulder and then knit the 22 sts from the front = 112 sts total. Work in pattern following Chart 1. So the garter st won't ruffle, BO somewhat tightly, preferably with a needle one size smaller than for body.

BLOCKING

Lay sweater, patted out to finished measurements, between two damp towels and leave until dry or very gently steam press under a damp pressing cloth.

TWISTED STITCH PONCHO

CO 368 sts; join, being careful not to twist cast-on row. Pm for beg of rnd. Work around in pattern following Chart 1. Next, work Chart 2, shaping at each side as follows:
Pm, p18, work 15 sts of pattern on Chart 2, p18, pm, k133, pm, p18, work 15 sts of pattern on Chart 2, p18, pm, k133.

RAGLAN SHAPING

Shape raglan as follows: Ssk at the beg of the St st section, knit until 2 sts rem on the St st section, k2tog. Rep the decreases in St st section of the other side = 4 sts decreased around. Dec the same way on every 4th rnd until the piece measures approx. 23¾ in / 60 cm = 266 sts rem. Finish as for the Sweater Poncho.

WRIST WARMERS

Left wrist warmer (worked back and forth):
With dpn, CO 47 sts. Work Chart 1 and then set up for hand:
Row 1: P6, work the 15 sts of pattern on Chart 2, p6, k20.
Row 2: P20, k6, work the 15 sts of pattern on Chart 2, k6.

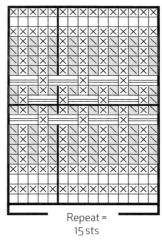

Chart 1

Repeat =
15 sts

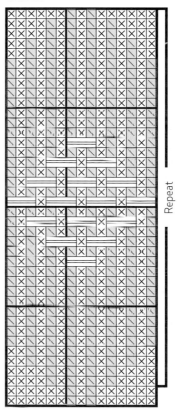

Chart 2

Repeat

Rep Rows 1-2 to end of Chart 2. Knit 4 rows in garter st.
So the garter st won't ruffle, BO somewhat tightly, preferably with a needle one size smaller.

Right wrist warmer (worked back and forth):
With dpn, CO 47 sts. Work Chart 1 and then set up for hand:
Row 1: K20, p6, work the 15 sts of pattern on Chart 2, p6.
Row 2: K6, work the 15 sts of pattern on Chart 2, k6, p20
Rep Rows 1-2 to end of Chart 2. Knit 4 rows in garter st.
So the garter st won't ruffle, BO somewhat tightly, preferably with a needle one size smaller.

FINISHING
Seam each cuff at the side, leaving an opening of about 1½ in / 4 cm; top of opening should be 2 in / 5 cm from bound-off row.

☐ Knit on RS, purl on WS
☒ Purl on RS, knit on WS
◩ Twisted knit on RS, twisted purl on WS
    (twisted st = work through back loop)

▤ Sl 3 sts to cn and hold in front of work.
    Wrap the yarn twice clockwise around the 3
    sts, sl sts back to left needle and knit them

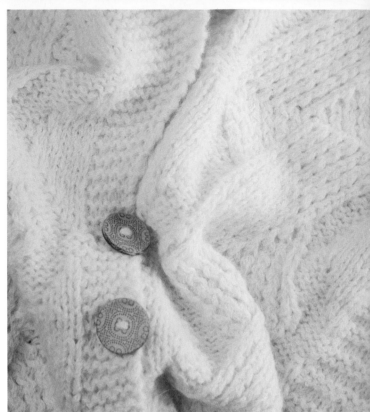

CAPE WITH OPTICAL ILLUSION CABLES

Design: Denise Samson

SIZES
S/M (L/XL)

MATERIALS
YARN: CYCA #5 (bulky) Hexa from Du Store Alpakka
(100% Merino wool; 109 yd/100 m / 50 g)
YARN AMOUNTS:
300 (350) g Natural White 910
NOTIONS: 3 large wooden buttons
NEEDLES: U.S. sizes 10½ or 11 / 7 mm, circular and set
of 5 dpn
GAUGE: 15 sts in St st = 4 in / 10 cm.
Adjust needle size to obtain correct gauge if necessary.
KNITTING TECHNIQUE: See chart on page 19
The cape is knitted in one piece. The pattern for

the optical illusion cable is easy to work and you
don't need a cable needle—the technique creates
the illusion that the stitches are crossed over
each other. The cape is worked back and forth.

CAPE

CO 72 sts (both sizes) and knit 6 rows in garter
stitch. Now work in charted pattern (see page 19)
until piece measures 2¾ in / 7 cm. Make a buttonhole: K2, BO 2 sts. On the next row, CO 2 sts over
the gap. Make another buttonhole when the piece
measures 5½ in / 14 cm and the third one at 8¼ in
/ 21 cm. Continue straight up in pattern as est until
piece is 9 in / 23 cm long. Now increase to shape
the collar: inc with M1 inside the edge st. Inc the
same way on every 4th row a total of 14 times—86
sts. Work the new sts in garter st. Continue over

all the sts until piece measures 29¼ (32) in / 74 (81) cm.

Now dec 1 st inside the edge st on every 4th row a total of 14 times = 72 sts rem. Work until there are a total of 9 (10) rep following the chart and end with 6 rows in garter st.

FINISHING
Weave in all ends neatly on WS. Sew on buttons.

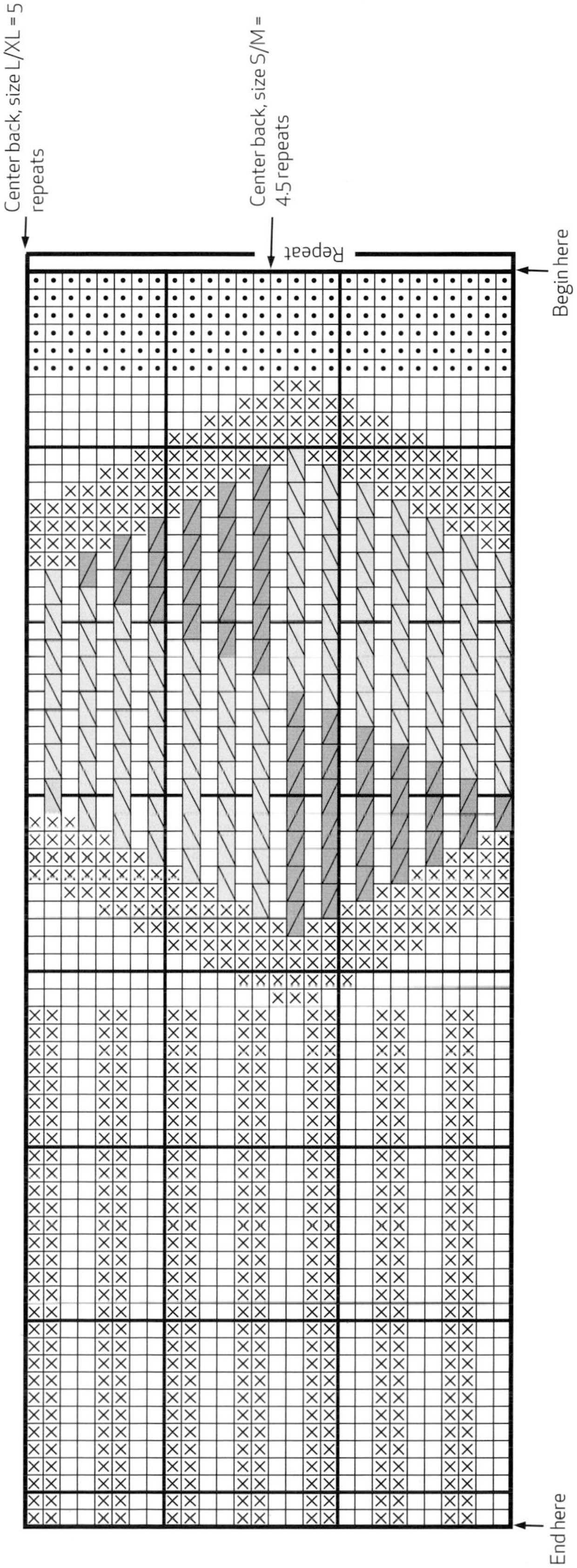

Center back, size L/XL = 5 repeats

Center back, size S/M = 4.5 repeats

Repeat

Begin here

End here

Legend:

- ⊡ Garter stitch (knit on RS, knit on WS)
- ☐ Knit on RS, purl on WS
- ☒ Purl on RS, knit on WS
- ◹ K2tog but do not slip from left needle; insert needle between the 2 sts and knit the 1st st. Sl both sts from needle.
- ◿ Knit the 2nd st on left needle through back loop but do not slip st from needle. Knit the 1st and 2nd sts together through back loops and slip both sts from needle.

LARGE PONCHO-SWEATER

Design: Sidsel J. Høivik

GAUGE: 12 sts in texture pattern on larger needles = 4 in / 10 cm.
Adjust needle sizes to obtain correct gauge if necessary.

SIZES

S/M (L, XL/XXL)

FINISHED MEASUREMENTS

WIDTH, FRONT AND BACK: 41¾ (45, 48) in / 106 (114, 122) cm

TOTAL LENGTH: 29½ (31½, 33½) in / 75 (80, 85) cm

SLEEVE LENGTH: 7 (7½, 8) in / 18 (19, 20) cm

MATERIALS

YARN: CYCA #6 (super bulky) Pus from Du Store Alpakka (70% alpaca, 17% acrylic, 13% nylon; 109 yd/100 m / 50 g)

YARN AMOUNTS:

COLOR 1: 50 (50, 100) g Beige 4009

COLOR 2: 300 (350, 400) g Light Blue 4019

COLOR 3: 300 (350, 400) g Dark Brown 4015

COLOR 4: 50 (50, 100) g Charcoal 4010

NEEDLES: U.S. sizes 11 / 8 mm, short circular and st of 5 dpn; U.S. size 13 / 9 mm, long circular

CROCHET HOOK: U.S. size K-10½ or L-11 / 7 mm

You're sure to be noticed in this fun poncho-sweater. It's worked with two colors, one for each section, with the yarns twisted around each other as for intarsia at the center. The scarf and hat with four colors of pompoms are the crowning touch! The front and back are worked separately going back and forth, and the sleeves are worked in the round.

BACK

With Color 1 and smaller circular, CO 120 (128, 136) sts. Working back and forth, knit 4 rows. Change to larger circular and work in pattern following the chart on page 23. *At the same time*, change colors. Half of the back is worked with Color 2 and the other half with Color 3; change colors at the center back.

Begin with Color 2 (see arrow on the chart) and work 60 (64, 68) sts with Color 3. When changing colors, begin at the arrow for CF = center front.

Throughout, make sure that you always work the center 2 sts (each in its own color) as knit on the RS and purl on WS. Work back and forth in the texture pattern following the chart, with both colors. Don't forget to twist the colors around each other on the WS on every row with a color change so that there won't be any holes at the changeover. Continue working back and forth as est until the back measures 28¾ (30¾, 32¼) in / 73 (78, 82) cm. BO the center 12 (14, 16) sts for back neck and work each side separately. When the piece measures 29½ (31½, 33½) in / 75 (80, 85) cm, BO rem sts rather loosely. BO with either 1 row k2, p2 or 1 row of St st. Make sure you also bind off the same way when you work the front so the pieces will match for finishing.

FRONT
Knit the front as for the back but work with the opposite colors after the bottom garter stitch edge. Begin with Color 3 at the right half and continue with Color 2 on the left half so that Color 2 ends at Color 2 and Color 3 adjoins Color 3 when the shoulders are joined.
When piece measures 26¾ (28¾, 30¾) in / 68 (73, 78) cm, BO the center 6 (8, 10) sts for the front neck. Work each shoulder separately, and, at neck edge, on every other row, bind off another 2-2-1-1 sts. When the piece is same length as for the back, BO rem sts as for back.

SLEEVES
With smaller dpn and Color 3, CO 24 (24, 24) sts; join, being careful not to twist cast-on row. (Purl 1 rnd, knit 1 rnd) 2 times and then purl 1 more rnd. Change to Color 4 and continue around in k2, p2 ribbing. Work in stripes, alternating 2 rnds Color 4 and 2 rnds Color 3. Pm at center of underarm (beg of rnd) and move the marker up every rnd. When sleeve is 1¼ in / 3 cm long, inc 1 st (with M1) on each side of the marker. Inc the same way about every 1½ in / 4 cm a total of 3 (3, 4) times. When the sleeve is 7 (7½, 8) in / 18 (19, 20) cm long or desired length, BO rather loosely.
Make the second sleeve the same way, but CO with Color 2 and work the garter st edge. Change to Color 4 and then alternate stripes of 2 rnds Color 4 and 2 rnds Color 2.

FINISHING
Seam the shoulders neatly.
Side edges: Use Color 2 along the side knitted with Color 3 and Color 3 along the side knitted with Color 2. With RS facing and smaller circular, pick up and knit 5-6 sts for every 2 in / 5 cm. Pick

up and knit stitches all along each side as well as along the garter section at lower edge. Knit 4 rows in garter st and then BO rather loosely knitwise on the next row (WS).
Neckband: With short, smaller circular and Color 1, pick up and knit about 6 sts for every 2 in / 5 cm. Join, pm for beg of rnd, and (purl 1rnd, knit 1 rnd) 2 times. BO rather loosely purlwise on the next rnd.

CROCHETED EDGINGS
Crochet as instructed below all around the sweater-poncho garter edges, lower edges of sleeves, and neckband. With Color 4, work around in sc spike st, each time inserting the hook into the space between the garter edge and the rest of the body. Work as follows: 1 sc, *ch 1, skip next st, 1 sc spike st*. Rep * to * around. In the outer corners, work 3 sc spike sts in the same place to round the corner. End the rnd with 1 sl st into the first stitch. Cut yarn.

Seam the sleeves neatly and firmly behind the garter edge. Loosely sew the seam at each side with about 4-6 / 10-15 cm length over from each sleeve. Weave in all ends neatly on WS.

Pompoms: Make a total of 12 pompoms with a 2-inch / 5-cm diameter, 3 of each color. Attach 3 pompoms of different colors at each corner, but do not attach too firmly—they need a little "wiggle" room.

HAT AND SCARF

FINISHED MEASUREMENTS
HAT:
CIRCUMFERENCE: approx. 20½ in / 52 cm
LENGTH: 12¾ in / 32 cm
SCARF:
WIDTH: 9¾ in / 25 cm
LENGTH: 78¾ in / 200 cm

MATERIALS
YARN: CYCA #6 (super bulky) Pus from Du Store
Alpakka (70% alpaca, 17% acrylic, 13% nylon; 109 yd/100
m / 50 g)
YARN AMOUNTS FOR HAT:
COLOR 1: 50 g Beige 4009
COLOR 2: 50 g Light Blue 4019
COLOR 3: 50 g Dark Brown 4015
COLOR 4: 50 g Charcoal 4010
YARN AMOUNTS FOR SCARF:
COLOR 1: 50 g Beige 4009
COLOR 2: 50 g Light Blue 4019
COLOR 3: 50 g Dark Brown 4015
COLOR 4: 50 g Charcoal 4010

NEEDLES: U.S. sizes 11 and 13 / 8 and 9 mm, short
circulars
CROCHET HOOK: U.S. size K-10½ or L-11 / 7-8 mm
GAUGE: 14 sts in ribbing or 12 sts in texture pattern on
larger needles = 4 in / 10 cm.
Adjust needle sizes to obtain correct gauge if necessary.

HAT
With Color 1 and smaller circular, CO 64 sts. Join,
being careful not to twist cast-on row; pm for beg
of rnd. The hat is worked in k2, p2 ribbing. Change
to larger circular and work 3¼ in / 8 cm with Color
4, 3¼ in / 8 cm with Color 3, and 3¼ in / 8 cm with
Color 2. BO rather loosely in ribbing. Lay the hat
flat and seam the top together.

Pompoms: Make a total of 6 pompoms, in various
colors, with a diameter of approx. 1¼–1½ in / 3–4
cm. Attach 3 pompoms of different colors at each
corner, but do not attach too firmly—they need a
little "wiggle" room.

SCARF
With Color 2 and larger needles, CO 36 sts. Work
back and forth in k2, p2 ribbing, always slipping
the first st of every row knitwise. When piece
is 19¾ in / 50 cm long, change to Color 1. When
scarf is 39½ in / 100 cm long, change to Color 3.
At 59 in / 150 cm, change to Color 4 and continue
until scarf is total length of 78¾ in / 200 cm. BO
loosely in k2, p2 ribbing. Cut yarn and weave in all
ends neatly on WS.

Pompoms: Make a total of 6 pompoms, in various
colors, with a diameter of approx. 2–5 cm. Sew
them evenly spaced along the cast-on and bound-
off edges.

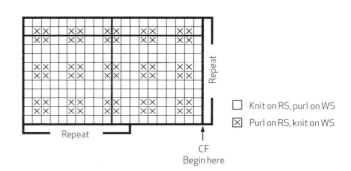

 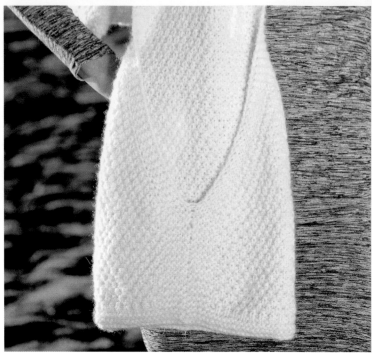

POCKET SCARF

Design: Hrönn Jónsdóttir

SIZES
S/M (L/XL)

FINISHED MEASUREMENTS
11¾ x 65 in (11¾ x 76¾) in / 30 x 165 (30 x 195) cm

MATERIALS
YARN: CYCA #6 (super bulky) Pus from Du Store Alpakka (70% alpaca, 17% acrylic, 13% nylon; 109 yd/100 m / 50 g)
YARN AMOUNTS:
300 (350) g White 4001
NEEDLES: U.S. size 10½ or 11 / 7 mm, short circular
GAUGE: 15 sts in texture pattern = 4 in / 10 cm.
Adjust needle size to obtain correct gauge if necessary.

———————————

This pocket scarf is multi-functional—you can wear it as a scarf, a vest, or a shawl. It's quick work on big needles! The scarf is worked both back and forth and in the round.

TEXTURE PATTERN
Row/Rnd 1: (K1, p1) across/around.

Row/Rnd 2: Work knit over knit and purl over purl.
Row/Rnd 3: (P1, k1) across/around.
Row/Rnd 4: Work knit over knit and purl over purl.
Rep Rows/Rnds 1–4.

CO 91 sts and join, being careful not to twist cast-on row. Pm for beg of rnd and work 7 rnds in garter stitch (alternate purl and knit rnds). Continue in texture pattern, keeping the first 5 and last 5 sts in garter st. When piece is about 6¼ / 16 cm long, divide the work at the beg of the rnd and work back and forth. Dec 1 st inside the 5 garter sts at each side on every other row until 45 sts rem. Dec with ssk at the beg of the row and k2tog at the end of the row. Continue without further shaping until the piece measures approx. 50¾ (62½) in / 129 (159) cm. Now inc 1 st inside the 5 garter sts at each side on every other row until there are 91 sts. Pm to measure the pocket from this point. Resume working in the round in texture pattern and garter st until pocket measures approx. 4¾ in / 12 cm. Work 7 rnds in garter st and then BO knitwise.

FINISHING
Fold the cast-on edge double and seam to close the pocket. Fold and seam the bound-off edge the same way. Weave in all ends neatly on WS.

PONCHO IN MISSONI STRIPES

Design: Denise Samson

The chevron stripes inspired by Missoni are always on the fashion scene! It's fun to knit stripes—you get hooked on seeing how the work develops with each color change. The poncho can be worn with the points at the front and back, or with the points at the sides. The garment is worked back and forth.

SIZES
S/M (L/XL)

FINISHED MEASUREMENTS
Approx. 23¾ x 56 in (26¾ x 64½) in / 60 x 144 (68 x 164) cm before finishing

MATERIALS
YARN: CYCA #2 (sport/baby) Royall Alpakka from Dale (100% alpaca; 145 yd/133 m / 50 g)

YARN AMOUNTS:

COLOR 1: 200 (250) g Light Mint 8231
COLOR 2: 150 (200) g Gray-blue 5813
COLOR 3: 150 (200) g Dove Blue 5931
NEEDLES: U.S. size 4 / 3.5 mm
GAUGE: 25 sts in pattern = 4 in / 10 cm.
Adjust needle size to obtain correct gauge if necessary.

STRIPE SEQUENCE
Work 12 rows with Color 1, 12 rows with Color 2, and 12 rows with Color 3.

With Color 1, CO 169 (193) sts and work back and forth in chevron pattern as follows:
Row 1: K1, *M1, k10, sl 1, k2tog, psso, k10, M1, k1*. Rep * to * across.
Row 2: Purl across.

Work the chevron pattern in the stripe sequence above until the piece measures approx. 56 (64½) in / 144 (164) cm. Make sure that you end with

Color 1. BO in pattern—inc and dec between the 10 knit sts as in pattern so the bound-off edge will maintain the wave shape.

FINISHING
Pin out the poncho to finished measurements and carefully steam press under a damp pressing cloth, making sure the wavy edges don't roll up.

Fold the piece into two = 28¼ (32¼) in / 72 (82) cm for each part. Measure 11¾ in / 30 cm from the fold and pm. With WS facing, use whip stitch to seam the piece, working through the outermost stitches so the seam will be smooth on the RS. Make sure the Color 3 (Dove Blue) stripes line up. See the sketch of Poncho 2 on page 6.

WRIST WARMERS
STRIPE SEQUENCE
Work 8 rows with Color 1, 8 rows with Color 2, and 8 rows with Color 3.
With Color 1, CO 49 sts and work back and forth in chevron pattern as follows:
Row 1: K1, *M1, k4, sl 1, k2tog, psso, k4, M1, k1*. Rep * to * across.
Row 2: Purl across.
Work a total of 2 color stripe repeats (or to desired length) of the chevron pattern in the stripe sequence above. BO as for poncho. Finish by seaming as for poncho.

KNITTING TIPS
If you think the wrist warmers will be a little too tight, you can add stitches at each end. For example, begin and end the row with k3 instead of k1 = total of 53 sts.

SQUARE PONCHO

SQUARE PONCHO

Design: Birte Aartun

SIZE
One size

FINISHED MEASUREMENTS
PONCHO BEFORE FINISHING: 15 x 32¾ in / approx. 38 x 83 cm

NECK CIRCUMFERENCE: approx. 28¼ in / 72 cm; length approx. 8¼ in / 21 cm

MATERIALS
YARN: CYCA #6 (super bulky) Pus from Du Store Alpakka (70% alpaca, 17% acrylic, 13% nylon; 109 yd/100 m / 50 g)

YARN AMOUNTS:

Version 1

COLOR 1: 200 g Blue 4004

COLOR 2: 100 g Denim 4003

COLOR 3: 100 g Light Blue 4019

Version 2

COLOR 1: 200 g Black 4017

COLOR 2: 100 g Dark Brown 4015

COLOR 3: 100 g Beige 4009

+ 1 spool Güterman's Sulky Glitter thread Yellow 6007

Yarn for Detached Collar

100 g Blue 4004 or Black 4017

NEEDLES: U.S. sizes 11 and 13 / 8 and 9 mm, very long circulars + short circular U.S. size 13 / 9 mm for detached collar

GAUGE: 12 sts in texture pattern on larger needles = 4 in / 10 cm.

Adjust needle sizes to obtain correct gauge if necessary.

You can wear this poncho two ways—with the points at the front and back, or with the points at the sides as shown in the photos. The poncho is worked back and forth. Why not make the matching detached collar for cold days?

TEXTURE PATTERN
Row 1 with Color 1: K2, (p2, k2) across.

Row 2 with Color 2: K2, (p2, k2) across.

Row 3 with Color 3: K2, (p2, k2) across

Rep Rows 1–3.

With Color 1 and smaller needles, CO 46 sts. Change to larger needles. Work back and forth in Texture pattern above until piece measures about 32¾ in / 83 cm. End with Row 1 of pattern and then BO knitwise with Color 1. Make another piece the same way.

FINISHING
Sew the pieces together as shown in Sketch 6 (page 7). While you sew, stretch the short ends slightly (the cast-on and bound-off edges), on the part sewn against the side edges. With Color 1 and smaller circular, pick up and knit sts along the lower edge, beginning and ending at center back. Pick up about 6-7 sts for every 2 in / 5 cm (the edge should be firm and "stretch out" the piece). Turn the piece with WS out, working twisted knits at the same time as you bind off. For the twisted knits, knit into back loop.

Knit the same edge around the neck opening. Weave in all ends neatly on WS.

Fringe at lower edge: Attach the fringe along the lower edge, spaced about 2 in / 5 cm apart. Make the fringe as follows: Cut 4 strands of Color 1 about 23¾ in / 60 cm long. Fold the bundle in half at the center to make a loop on one end. Use a crochet hook to bring the loop up from the WS to the RS of the lower edge until the loop is large enough that you can insert your thumb or index finger through it. Bring all 8 strands through the loop and tighten until the loop closes. When all the fringes have been attached, knot them together. Take 4 strands from each fringe and make a knot about 1½ in / 4 cm down on the strand. Finish by trimming the fringe with sharp scissors to a similar length (about 5½ in / 14 cm below the knot). See page 51 for a close-up of the fringe.

DETACHED RIBBED COLLAR
With Blue or Black and larger
short circular, CO 88 sts.
Join, being careful not to
twist cast-on row; pm for
beg of rnd. Knit around in
k2, p2 ribbing until piece is
about 8¼ in / 21 cm long.
BO in ribbing. Weave in
all ends neatly on WS.

CLASSIC CABLED PONCHO

Design: Denise Samson

SIZES

S/M (L/XL)

FINISHED MEASUREMENTS

approx. 17¾ x 59 (21¼ x 63) in / 45 x 150 (54 x 160) cm

MATERIALS

YARN: CYCA #3 (DK/light worsted) Sterk from Du Store Alpakka (40% Merino wool, 40% alpaca, 20% polyamide; 150 yd/137 m / 50 g)

YARN AMOUNTS:

500 (600) g White 851

NOTIONS: 3 small round mother-of-pearl buttons

NEEDLES: U.S. size 4 / 3.5 mm; cable needle

CROCHET HOOK: U.S. size D-3 / 3 mm

GAUGE: 22 sts in St st = 4 in / 10 cm.

Adjust needle size to obtain correct gauge if necessary.

You can wear this pretty poncho just as well with a dressy skirt or scruffy pants. It is worked back and forth in one long piece except for the neckband which is worked in the round. The three small mother-of-pearl buttons at the top of the V-neck provide a special little touch.

PONCHO

CO 128 (156) sts and work in pattern as follows:

PATTERN, SIZE S/M

P2, Cable C with 8 sts, p2, k8, p2, Cable B with 16 sts, p2, k8, p2, Cable A with 8 sts, p2, k8, p2, Cable C with 8 sts, p2, k8, p2, Cable B with 16 sts, p2, k8, p2, Cable A with 8 sts, p2.

Continue as est until piece measures about 59

Cable A

8 sts · Repeat

Cable B

16 sts · Repeat

Cable C

8 sts · Repeat

[top to bottom here = from left to right on chart]

P2 · Cable B · P2 · K8 · P2 · Cable A · P2 · K8 · P2 · Cable B · P2 · K8 · P2 · Cable C · P2 · K8 · P2 · Cable A · P2 · K8 · P2 · Cable B · P2 · K8 · P2 · Cable C · P2

Rep until piece measures approx. 59 (63) in / 150 (160) cm

S/M 128 sts

L/XL 156 sts

☐ Knit on RS, purl on WS

☒ Purl on RS, knit on WS

⬭ Sl 2 sts to cable needle and hold in front of work, k2, k2 from cable needle

⬭ Sl 2 sts to cable needle and hold in back of work, k2, k2 from cable needle

in / 150 cm long. Make sure that you end with a complete repeat.

SIZE L/XL

P2, Cable C with 8 sts, p2, k8, p2, Cable B with 16 sts, p2, k8, p2, Cable A with 8 sts, p2, k8, p2, Cable C with 8 sts, p2, k8, p2, Cable B with 16 sts, p2, k8, p2, Cable A with 8 sts, p2, k8, p2, Cable B with 16 sts, p2.

Continue as est until piece measures about 63 in / 160 cm long. Make sure that you end with a complete repeat.

FINISHING

Carefully steam press garment under a damp pressing cloth or lay between two damp towels; leave until dry.
Fold the short side against the long side so the shape of the poncho is rounded at the back and has a point at the front, and so you have an opening for the head (see sketch on page 6). Seam smoothly—the seam should be approx. 21¼ (25¼) in / 54 (64) cm long.

NOTE: If you knitted the L/XL size, make sure you finish the poncho in such a way as to have a narrow cable (Cable C) around the V-neck and back neck.

NECKBAND

Pick up and knit 1 st in V at center front; continue to pick up and knit sts all around the neck in the outermost st of the narrow cables. In each cable, pick up and knit 5 sts in each cable for every 6 sts in cable. Pm after 51 sts (do not count center st), pick up and knit 30 sts, pm, pick up and knit 64 sts, pm, pick up and knit 30 sts, pm, pick up and knit 51 sts. Now work around as follows:

K1 (center st), k2tog, knit to 1st marker, slm, ssk, knit until 2 sts before next marker, k2tog, slm. Knit to next marker, slm, ssk, knit until 2 sts before next marker, k2tog, slm. Knit until 2 sts before marker at center st, ssk.

Decrease the same way on every round a total of 16 times. BO loosely, leaving the last loop on the needle.
Sl the last st to crochet hook and work 1 rnd sc with 1 sc in each st along the left side. Along back neck, skip every 3rd st by working 2 sc tog, skip 1 st, until you come to the right side. Work 1 sc in each st. Join the last st to the center st with 1 sl st. Now work a round of crab st (sc worked from left to right) and join last st with sl st to first st.

Carefully steam press neckband under a damp pressing cloth. Sew the three mother-of-pearl buttons at center front in the V.

PONCHO WITH LEAF MOTIFS

Design: Denise Samson

SIZE
One size

FINISHED MEASUREMENTS
approx. 25¼ x 51¼) in / 64 x 130) cm before finishing

MATERIALS
YARN: CYCA #3 (DK/light worsted) Ensemble Glitter Light from Artyarns (50% silk, 50% cashmere and lurex; 400 yd/366 m / 80 g)
YARN AMOUNTS:
3 skeins White 250
NEEDLES: U.S. size 4 / 3.5 mm; cable needle
CROCHET HOOK: U.S. size C-2 / 2.5 mm
GAUGE: 18 sts = 4 in / 10 cm.
Adjust needle size to obtain correct gauge if necessary.

For this dressy poncho, I chose an exclusive yarn spun with silk and cashmere. It's so light that the whole poncho only used 8.04 oz / 228 g! The garment is worked back and forth.

PONCHO
CO 156 sts and knit 1 row (= WS). Continue in pattern following Chart 1 until piece measures 51¼ in / 130 cm. BO.

FINISHING
Pin out the edges of the piece and gently steam press under a damp pressing cloth so that the leaves make waves along the edges. Carefully steam press the entire piece under a damp pressing cloth.

Fold the short end against the long side so the poncho is rounded on one side and has a point on the other. Make sure to leave an opening for the head (see sketch on page 6). Neatly sew the seam

(the seam should be about 23¾ in / 60 cm long). You can decide whether you prefer the point at the front or back.

WRIST WARMERS
CO 54 sts and knit 1 row (= WS). Working back and forth, continue in pattern following Chart 2. When piece is 4¾ in / 12 cm long, M1 in each purl section = 58 sts. Continue in pattern until piece is 6¼ in / 16 cm long. M1 in each purl section = 62 sts. Work as est until piece is 8¾ in / 22 cm long. BO.

FINISHING
Seam the side of each wrist warmer, but, when 1½ in / 4 cm down from bound-off row, leave an opening about 1¼ in / 3 cm long for the thumb. See sketch on page 6.

EDGINGS
Crochet a picot edge at the top and bottom of each wrist warmer.
Picot: *Ch 3, 1 sc in the first of the 3 ch, skip 1 st and work 1 sl st into next st*. Rep * to * around and end with 1 sl st into 1st of the 3 ch at beg of rnd.

Work 1 rnd sc around each thumbhole.

Chart 1

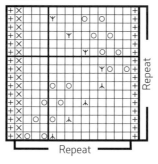

Repeat

Chart 2

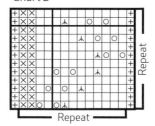

Repeat

⊞	Edge st = knit on RS, knit on WS
☐	Knit on RS, purl on WS
⊠	Purl on RS, knit on WS
◉	Yarnover
Ⴤ	Sl 1, k2tog, psso
⅄	K3tog

CROCHETED FOUR-LEAFED CLOVER PONCHO

Design: Denise Samson

This crocheted poncho is made with a total of 192 squares, joined into two larger pieces. The pattern is reversible and can be worked in many types of yarn. It takes some patience to crochet so many identical squares, but the results are so fine that it'll be totally worth it!

SIZE
One size

FINISHED MEASUREMENTS
Each piece measures: 17¼ x 29½ in / 44 x 75 cm
Total length: 30 in / 76 cm

MATERIALS
YARN: CYCA #2 (sport/baby) Cotton Viscose from Drops (54% cotton, 46% rayon/viscose; 120 yd/110 m / 50 g)
YARN AMOUNTS:
450 g Denim 22
CROCHET HOOK: U.S. size G-6 / 4 mm
GAUGE: Each square measures 2 x 2 in / 5 x 5 cm. Adjust hook size to obtain correct gauge if necessary.

CROCHETED SQUARE
Ch 8 and join into a ring with 1 sl st into first ch.
Rnd 1: Work 16 sc around ring and join rnd with 1 sl st into first ch.
Rnd 2: *Ch 9, skip 3 sts, 1 sc*. Rep * to * around = 4 ch loops.
Rnd 3: *1 sl st, (3 sc, ch 3) 3 times, 3 sc*. Rep * to * in each ch loop.

You can sew or crochet the squares together in the 1st and 3rd picots (ch loops) of the 3rd rnd to make a cross between four crocheted squares. You should make two matching pieces with 8 squares across and 12 squares in length = 96 squares for each piece. Join the short side of one piece to the long side of the other piece and do the same on the opposite side so that you have an opening for the head and a point at both front and back. See the sketch on page 42.

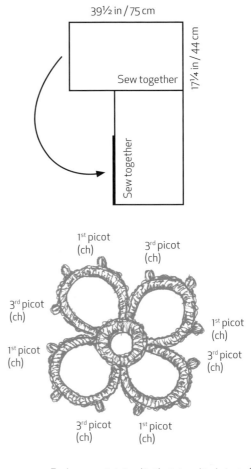

39½ in / 75 cm

17¼ in / 44 cm

Sew together

Sew together

1st picot
(ch)

3rd picot
(ch)

3rd picot
(ch)

1st picot
(ch)

1st picot
(ch)

3rd picot
(ch)

3rd picot
(ch)

1st picot
(ch)

Each square is joined in the 1st and 3rd picots (ch).

BARCELONA PONCHO/CABLED SHAWL

Design: A Knit Story

The Barcelona poncho was inspired by Catalonia's capital, one of the world's most charming large cities. It combines a mild Mediterranean climate with world-class art and night life. The poncho can be worn in several different ways. It's worked back and forth.

SIZE
One size

FINISHED MEASUREMENTS
23¾ x 67¾ in / 60 x 172 cm

MATERIALS
YARN: CYCA #5 (chunky/craft/rug) Brushed Baby Alpaca from A Knit Story (100% alpaca; 96 yd/ 88 m / 25 g)

YARN AMOUNTS:
Approx. 500 g Charcoal

NOTIONS: 6 small buttons

NEEDLES: U.S. size 8 / 5 mm; cable needle

GAUGE: 16 sts in St st = 4 in / 10 cm.
Adjust needle size to obtain correct gauge if necessary.

PONCHO/SHAWL
CO 103 sts and work back and forth in k3, p2 ribbing for 3½ in / 9 cm. Now continue in pattern:

Row 1 (RS): K3, p2, inc 4 sts evenly spaced over the next 23 sts (= 27 knit sts), p2, knit until 5 sts rem and end with p2, k3.

Row 2: P3, k2, purl until 34 sts rem, k2, p27, k2, p3.

Row 3: K3, p2, k27, p2, knit until 5 sts rem and end with p2, k3.

CABLE
C27F: P2, k9, sl 9 sts to cn and hold in front, k9, k9 from cn, p2.

44

6 buttonholes, 4 in / 10 cm apart

C27B: P2, sl 9 sts to cn and hold in back, k9, k9 from cn, k9, p2.

Follow chart from C1 to C15 and, at the same time, make 6 buttonholes on the side opposite the cables (see next page for buttonhole instructions).

Repeat the 2nd and 3rd rows of the pattern for 2½ in / 6 cm until the piece measures 6 in / 15 cm from the cast-on row (end with Row 2).

Cable 1: Work C27F and then knit until 5 sts rem; end with p2, k3.
Rep Rows 2–3 for 3¼ in / 8 cm—the piece measures 9 in / 23 cm from the cast-on row. End with Row 2.
Cable 2: Work C27B and then knit until 5 sts rem; end with p2, k3.
Rep Rows 2–3 for 4¾ in / 12 cm—the piece measures 13¾ in / 35 cm from the cast-on row. End with Row 2.

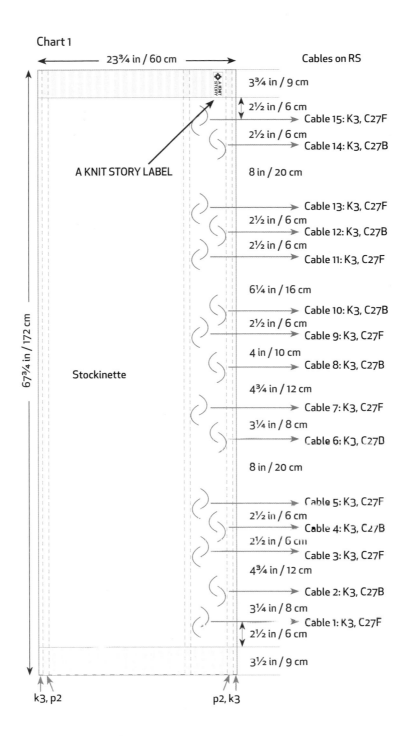

Chart 1

23¾ in / 60 cm

Cables on RS

3¾ in / 9 cm

2½ in / 6 cm

Cable 15: K3, C27F

2½ in / 6 cm

Cable 14: K3, C27B

8 in / 20 cm

A KNIT STORY LABEL

Cable 13: K3, C27F

2½ in / 6 cm

Cable 12: K3, C27B

2½ in / 6 cm

Cable 11: K3, C27F

6¼ in / 16 cm

Cable 10: K3, C27B

2½ in / 6 cm

Cable 9: K3, C27F

4 in / 10 cm

Cable 8: K3, C27B

4¾ in / 12 cm

Cable 7: K3, C27F

3¼ in / 8 cm

Cable 6: K3, C27D

8 in / 20 cm

Cable 5: K3, C27F

2½ in / 6 cm

Cable 4: K3, C27B

2½ in / 6 cm

Cable 3: K3, C27F

4¾ in / 12 cm

Cable 2: K3, C27B

3¼ in / 8 cm

Cable 1: K3, C27F

2½ in / 6 cm

3½ in / 9 cm

67¾ in / 172 cm

Stockinette

k3, p2

p2, k3

Cable 3: Work C27F and then knit until 5 sts rem; end with p2, k3.

Continue, working as shown on the chart through Cable 15. Rep Rows 2–3 for 2½ in / 6 cm. On the last row, dec 4 sts spaced evenly across the 27 cable sts (= 23 knit sts rem). End with 3½ in / 9 cm in k3, p2 ribbing. BO in ribbing. The piece should measure 67¾ in / 172 cm.

Buttonholes: Make 6 buttonholes on the side opposite the cables. Every 4 in / 10 cm, with RS facing, BO the first of the two purl sts on the needle. On the next, WS, row, CO 2 sts over the gap.

FINISHING

Sew buttons opposite buttonholes. Weave in all ends neatly on WS. Sew on the A KNIT STORY label as shown on Chart 1.

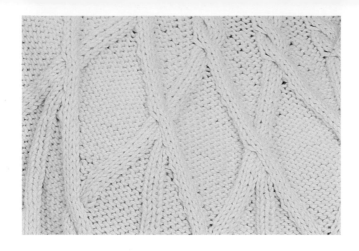

PONCHO WITH SHORT ROLLED COLLAR

Design: Turid Stapnes

SIZE
One size

FINISHED MEASUREMENTS
CIRCUMFERENCE AT CHEST: approx. 63 in /160 cm
CIRCUMFERENCE AT LOWER EDGE: approx. 98½ in /
250 cm
TOTAL LENGTH: 27½ in / 70 cm

MATERIALS
YARN: CYCA #4 (worsted/afghan/Aran) Vår from Viking
of Norway (100% cotton; 93 yd/85 m / 50 g)
YARN AMOUNTS:
1050 g Natural White 402
NEEDLES: U.S. sizes 4 / 3.5 mm, short circular and set
of 5 dpn; U.S. 6 / 4 mm, long and short circulars; cable
needle
GAUGE: 20 sts in St st on larger needle = 4 in /10 cm.
Adjust needle sizes to obtain correct gauge if necessary.

————————

Here's a pretty sweater-poncho in a 100% cotton
yarn. The yarn is soft and lovely to knit with for a
beautiful garment to span the shift from spring to
summer. It's knit in the round; change to shorter
length circulars as necessary.

PONCHO
With larger long circular, CO 576 sts. Join, being
careful not to twist cast-on row; pm for beg of
rnd. Work around following Chart 1. Decrease as
shown on the chart. After completing charted
rows, 384 sts rem. Now work following Chart 2,
decreasing as shown on chart = 96 sts rem.

NECKBAND
Change to smaller circular and work around in k1,
p1 ribbing for 4¾ in / 12 cm. Loosely BO in ribbing.

CUFFS
With smaller dpn, CO 48 sts. Join; pm for beg of
rnd. Work 4 garter ridges (1 ridge = knit 1 rnd, purl
1 rnd). Knit next rnd, increasing evenly spaced
around to 64 sts. Now work following Chart 3
until piece measures approx. 7 in /18 cm, ending
as shown on the chart = 48 sts rem. Work 4 garter
ridges (= 8 rnds). BO.
Make the second cuff the same way.

FINISHING
Sew the cuffs to the poncho along the cast-on
edge at each side. Weave in all ends neatly on WS.

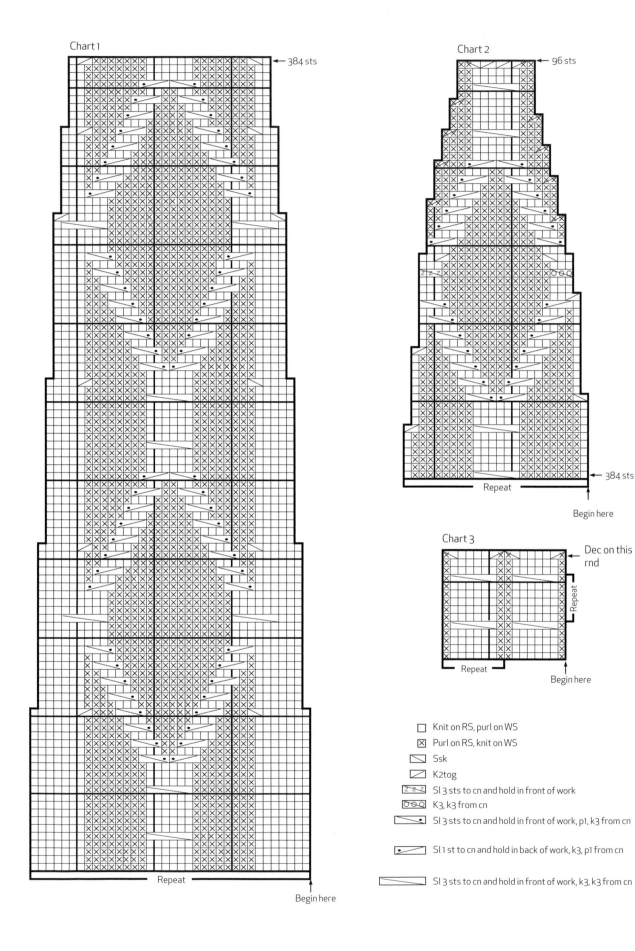

Chart 1

← 384 sts

Begin here

Repeat

Chart 2

← 96 sts

Repeat

← 384 sts

Begin here

Chart 3

Dec on this rnd

Repeat

Repeat

Begin here

☐ Knit on RS, purl on WS

☒ Purl on RS, knit on WS

◹ Ssk

◸ K2tog

⊠⊠⊠ Sl 3 sts to cn and hold in front of work

○○○ K3, k3 from cn

⟍• Sl 3 sts to cn and hold in front of work, p1, k3 from cn

•⟋ Sl 1 st to cn and hold in back of work, k3, p1 from cn

▱ Sl 3 sts to cn and hold in front of work, k3, k3 from cn

CABLE-KNIT SQUARE PONCHO

Design: Birte Aartun

GAUGE: 12 sts in texture pattern on larger needles = 4 in / 10 cm.
Adjust needle sizes to obtain correct gauge if necessary.

SIZE
One size

FINISHED MEASUREMENTS
EACH PIECE, BEFORE FINISHING: 15 x 32¾ in / approx. 38 x 83 cm
NECK CIRCUMFERENCE: approx. 27½ in / 80 cm; length approx. 8¼ in / 21 cm

MATERIALS
YARN: CYCA #6 (super bulky) Pus from Du Store Alpakka (70% alpaca, 17% acrylic, 13% nylon; 109 yd/ 100 m / 50 g)
YARN AMOUNTS:
350 g Light Blue 4019
NOTIONS: 4 large baby blue heart-shaped mother-of-pearl buttons
NEEDLES: U.S. sizes 11 and 13 / 8 and 9 mm, very long circulars; cable needle

Here's a comfy poncho knitted in a heavy alpaca yarn with slipped stitches for a woven look, cables, and fringe. A veritable cornucopia of a poncho! It's made with two matching pieces, knitted back and forth.

PONCHO

With smaller circular, CO 52 sts. Change to larger circular and work back and forth in pattern following the chart on page 53. The 1st row = RS. When piece is approx. 32¾ in / 83 cm long, BO, but, *at the same time*, k2tog 4 times over the cable sts. Make a second piece the same way.

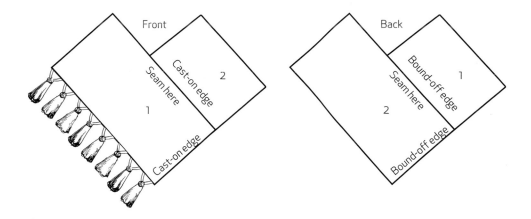

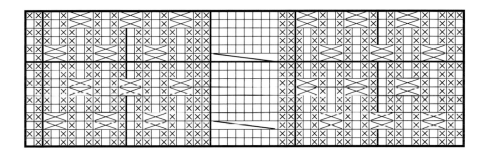

☐   Knit on RS, purl on WS

☒   Purl on RS, knit on WS

⊠   Weave pattern: Sl 3 sts purlwise with yarn held in front of work on RS or in back on WS as appropriate

⬭   Sl 4 sts to cn and hold in front of work, k4, k4 from cn

FINISHING

Join the pieces as shown on the sketch on page 53, stretching the short ends (the cast-on and bound-off edges) slightly to ease in when sewing to the side edges.

EDGINGS:

With smaller circular, pick up and knit sts along lower edge, beginning and ending at center back. Pick up and knit about 6-7 sts for every 2 in / 5 cm (the edge should be a bit tight and pull in the piece somewhat). Turn work so WS faces and BO across, knitting all sts through back loops. Work the edgings around the front and back necks the same way.

FRINGE ALONG LOWER EDGE:

Space fringes about 2 in / 5 cm apart along the lower edge. Make the fringes as follows:
Cut 4 strands of Color 1 about 23¾ in / 60 cm long. Fold the bundle in half at the center to make a loop on one end. Use a crochet hook to bring the loop up from the WS to the RS of the lower edge until the loop is large enough that you can insert your thumb or index finger through it. Bring all 8 strands through the loop and tighten until the loop closes. When all the fringes have been attached, knot them together. Take 4 strands from each fringe and make a knot about 1½ in / 4 cm down on the strand. Finish by trimming the fringe with sharp scissors to a similar length (about 5½ in / 14 cm below the knot). Sew on the decorative buttons.

PONCHO CROCHETED WITH BLOCKS OF STARS

Design: May Britt Bjella Zamori

SIZE
One size

FINISHED MEASUREMENTS
Length at center front, when worn on diagonal: approx.
37½ in / 95 cm

MATERIALS
YARN: CYCA #3 (DK/light worsted) Lerke from Dale
(52% Merino wool, 48% cotton; 125 yd/114 m / 50 g)
YARN AMOUNTS:
500 g Slate 5752
CROCHET HOOK: U.S. size G-6 / 4 mm
GAUGE: Small square = 4¾ x 4¾ in / 12 x 12 cm; large
square 9½ x 9½ in / 24 x 24 cm
Adjust hook size to obtain correct gauge if necessary.

SPECIAL ABBREVIATION: tr cl = treble cluster = 3 or 4
tr joined together (work each tr up to but not including
last step and then join when all specified tr have been
worked).

A large and light poncho crocheted with an airy
blend of Merino wool and cotton. The squares are
joined by crocheting them together on the last
round.

SMALL SQUARE
Ch 6; join into a ring with 1 sl st into 1st ch.

Rnd 1: Ch 8 (= 1 dc + 5 ch), work (1 dc around ring,
ch 5) 6 times, 1 dc around ring, ch 1, 1 tr in 3rd ch =
8 loops.

Rnd 2: Ch 3, 3-tr cl in ch loop, ch 7, (4-tr cl in next ch-5 loop, ch 7) 6 times, 4-tr cl in next ch-5 loop, ch 3, 1 tr in 1st tr-cl.

Rnd 3: Ch 1, 1 sc in tr, *ch 5, (1 dc, ch 5, 1 tr, ch 5, 1 tr, ch 5, 1 dc) in next ch-7 loop, ch 5, 1 sc in next ch-7 loop*. Rep * to * 4 times, ending last rep with 1 sl st into 1st sc instead of 1 sc in ch-7 loop.

Rnd 4: 1 sl st into first ch-5 loop, ch 3, 2 dc in same ch loop, ch 1, *(3 dc, ch 1) in next ch-5 loop, (3 dc, ch 3, 3 dc) in next ch-5 loop, (3 dc, ch 1) in next three ch-5 loops*. Rep * to * 3 times, (3 dc, ch 1) in next ch-5 loop, (3 dc, ch 3, 3 dc) in next ch-5 loop, (3 dc, ch 1) in next two ch-5 loops. End with 1 sl st into 1st dc.

LARGE SQUARE

Ch 6; join into a ring with 1 sl st into 1st ch.

Rnd 1: Ch 8 (= 1 dc + 5 ch), work *1 dc around ring, ch 5*; rep * to *7 times, 1 sl st in 3rd ch.

Rnd 2: 1 sl st in first ch-5 loop, ch 3, 5 dc around same ch-loop, *6 dc in next ch-5 loop*; rep * to *7 times, 1 sl st into 3rd ch.

Rnd 3: 1 sl st into next dc, ch 3, 3-tr cl over the next 3 dc, ch 9, skip 2 dc, *4 tr tr cl over next 4 dc, ch 9, skip 2 dc*; rep * to *6 times, 4 tr cl over the next 4 dc, ch 5, 1 tr in 1st tr cl.

Rnd 4: Ch 1, 1 sc in tr, *ch 7, (1 dc, ch 7, 1 tr, ch 7, 1 tr, ch 7, 1 dc) around next ch-9 loop, ch 7, 1 sc in next ch-9 loop*; rep * to * 4 times but end with 1 sl st into 1st sc instead of 1 sc in ch-9 loop.

Rnd 5: 1 sl st into ch-7 loop, ch 3, 2 dc in same ch loop, ch 1, *(3 dc, ch 1, 3 dc, ch 1) in next ch-7 loop, (3 dc, ch 3, 3 dc) in next ch-7 loop, *(3 dc, ch 1, 3 dc, ch 1) in each of next three 7-c loops*; rep * to * 3 times, (3 ch, ch 1) in next ch-7 loop, (3 dc, ch 3, 3 dc) in next ch-7 loop, (3 dc, ch 1) in next two ch-7 loops; end with 1 sl st into 1st dc.

Rnd 6: 1 sl st back in ch-1 loop, ch 1, *(1 sc in ch-1 loop, ch 6) 5 times, (1 sc, ch 6, 1 sc) in ch-3 loop, ch 6, (1 sc in ch-1 loop, ch 6) 4 times*; rep * to * 4 times but end last rep with ch 3 and 1 dc in 1st sc instead of last ch 6.

Rnd 7: Ch 1 *(1 sc in ch-6 loop, ch 6) 6 times, (1 sc, ch 6, 1 sc) in next ch-6 loop, (ch 6, 1 sc in next ch-6 loop) 5 times*; rep * to * 4 times, but end with ch 3 and 1 dc in 1st sc instead of last ch-6 loop.

Rnd 8: 1 sl st into ch loop, ch 3, 1 dc in same ch loop, *(ch 1, 3 dc in next ch-6 loop) 5 times, (3 dc, ch 3, 3 dc) in next ch-6 loop, (ch 1, 3 dc in next ch-6 loop) 6 times*; rep * to * 4 times but end with 1 dc around last ch-6 loop and 1 sl st into 3rd ch.

Joining the squares: On the last round, work 1 sc in the corresponding ch-1 loop of the previous square instead of ch 1.

Crochet to join the 2 large and 52 small squares following the schematic below.

FINISHING

Weave in all ends neatly on WS. Fold the piece at the center = the dotted line on schematic. Place A against A and B against B and either sew or crochet together the 3 squares between a and b.

EDGING

Beginning at one corner, work all around the poncho; attach yarn with 1 sl st.

Rnd 1: Ch 1, *(1 sc, ch 5, 1 sc) in the corner loop, (ch 5, 1 sc in next ch-1 loop) to the next corner*; rep * to * 4 times and join with 1 sl st into 1st sc.

Rnd 2: 1 sl st into the ch-5 loop, (ch 3, 2 dc, ch 1, 3 dc) in corner loop, *(3 dc, ch 1 in next ch-5 loop) to next corner loop, (3 dc, ch 1, 3 dc) in corner loop*; rep * to * 3 times, (3 dc, ch 1 in next ch-5 loop) to next corner loop, 1 sl st into 3rd ch.

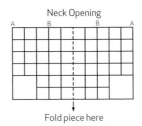

Neck Opening

Fold piece here

NEW YORK SKYLINE PONCHO

Design: A Knit Story

SIZE
One size

FINISHED MEASUREMENTS
23¾ x 67 in / 60 x 170 cm

MATERIALS
YARN: CYCA #5 (chunky/craft/rug) Brushed Baby Alpaca from A Knit Story (100% alpaca; 96 yd/88 m / 25 g)
YARN AMOUNTS:
300 g Light Gray
300 g Lead Gray
NOTIONS: 6 buttons
NEEDLES: U.S. size 8 / 5 mm
GAUGE: 16 sts in St st = 4 in / 10 cm.
Adjust needle size to obtain correct gauge if necessary.

This cozy poncho was inspired by New York's skyline. It's knitted with the softest baby alpaca in two lovely shades of gray. The poncho is made in one piece worked back and forth.

PONCHO

With Light Gray, loosely CO 97 sts. Work 3¼ in / 8 cm in ribbing: K1 (edge st), (k1, p1) to last 2 sts and end with k1, k1 (edge st). Continue in stripe pattern, which consists of St st in the main color and half brioche (fisherman's rib) in the contrast color, following the chart on page 60, and with a 5-st band at each side: K1 edge st, k1, p1, k1, p1 at beg of row and p1, k1, p1, k1, edge st at end of row. On the right band, make 6 buttonholes as follows: k1 edge st, k1, p1, yo, k2tog. On the next row, k1 into the yarnover. Place the first buttonhole at 4 in / 10 cm from cast-on and then space the rem 5 buttonholes 4 in / 10 cm apart. End with 3¼ in / 8 cm ribbing as for beg of poncho. BO somewhat loosely in ribbing.

Chart 1

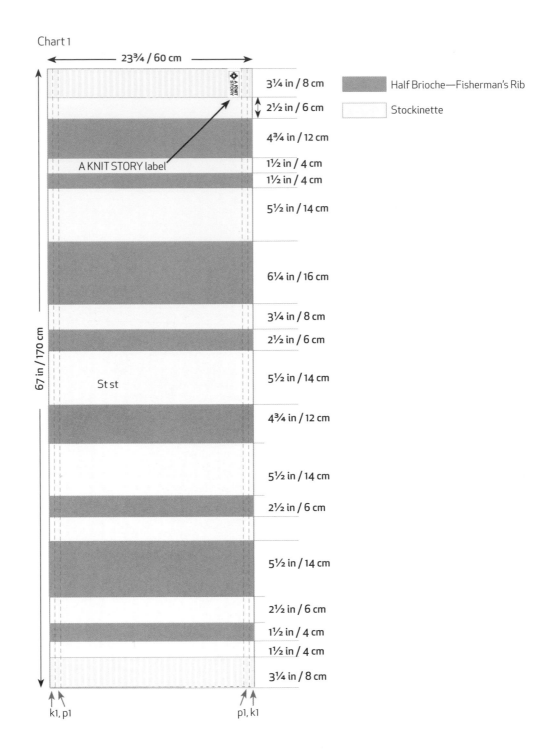

23¾ / 60 cm

3¼ in / 8 cm

2½ in / 6 cm

4¾ in / 12 cm

A KNIT STORY label

1½ in / 4 cm

1½ in / 4 cm

5½ in / 14 cm

6¼ in / 16 cm

3¼ in / 8 cm

2½ in / 6 cm

5½ in / 14 cm

4¾ in / 12 cm

5½ in / 14 cm

2½ in / 6 cm

5½ in / 14 cm

2½ in / 6 cm

1½ in / 4 cm

1½ in / 4 cm

3¼ in / 8 cm

67 in / 170 cm

St st

k1, p1

p1, k1

Half Brioche—Fisherman's Rib

Stockinette

HALF BRIOCHE—FISHERMAN'S RIB

Row 1 (RS): (K1 in st below next st on needle, p1) across.

Row 2 (WS): Knit across.

FINISHING

Sew on buttons opposite buttonholes. Weave in all ends neatly on WS. Sew on A KNIT STORY label as shown on Chart 1.

PONCHO WITH CABLES AND BELT OPENINGS

Design: Hrönn Jónsdóttir

SIZES
S/M (L/XL)

FINISHED MEASUREMENTS
CHEST: 72½ (78¾) in / 184 (200) cm
TOTAL LENGTH: 28 (29½) in / 71 (75) cm

MATERIALS
YARN: CYCA #6 (super bulky) Pus from Du Store
Alpakka (70% alpaca, 17% acrylic, 13% nylon; 109 yd/100 m / 50 g)
YARN AMOUNTS:
550 (600) g Light Gray 4011
NEEDLES: U.S. size 11 / 8 mm, short circular and set of 5 dpn; U.S. size 13 / 9 mm, very long circular; cable needle
GAUGE: 14 sts in pattern on larger needles = 4 in / 10 cm. Adjust needle sizes to obtain correct gauge if necessary.

———————————

This square poncho features large cables and openings for a wide belt. The garment is worked back and forth except for the neckband which is worked in the round. The belt holds the poncho in place so you don't have any sewing up to do.

Edge stitch: Sl 1 purlwise with yarn in front at beg of row and k1 at end of row.

FRONT
With larger needles, CO 131 (143) sts. Work in k1, p1

ribbing inside the edge sts at each side until piece measures approx. 1¼ in / 3 cm. On the last row, decrease 1 st = 130 (142) sts. Continue in charted pattern except for 5 sts at each side which continue in ribbing and edge st as est. When piece measures 9¾ in / 25 cm, make the belt openings: Work back and forth over the first 41 sts for about 4 in / 10 cm. Cut yarn and reattach to work back and forth over the center 48 (60) sts for 4 in / 10 cm. Cut yarn and reattach to work the last 41 sts for 4 in / 10 cm. Now work over all the sts across until piece measures approx. 25¼ (26¾) in / 64 (68) cm. Shape the shoulders by binding off from the armhole side inwards: 22-6-6-5-4-4 (26-6-6-6-5-4) sts at each side. Place the rem 36 center sts on a holder.

BACK
Work as for the front.

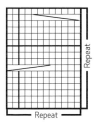

□   Knit on RS, purl on WS

▱   Sl 4 sts to cn and hold in front of work, k4, k4 from cn

▱   Sl 4 sts to cn and hold in back of work, k4, k4 from cn

NECKBAND
Join the shoulders. Place the 36 sts from each holder on smaller circular. Join and pm for beg of rnd. Work around in k1, p1 ribbing for ¾ in / 2 cm. BO in ribbing. Weave in all ends neatly on WS.

BELL-SHAPED PONCHO

Design: Sidsel J. Høivik

SIZES
S (M, L)

FINISHED MEASUREMENTS
TOTAL LENGTH: approx. 28¼ (30, 31½) in / 72 (76, 80) cm

MATERIALS
YARN: CYCA #1 (fingering) Tynn Alpakka from Du Store Alpakka (100% alpaca; 183 yd/167 m / 50 g)
AND CYCA #1 (fingering) Air from Du Store Alpakka (78% Suri alpaca, 22% nylon; 257 yd/ 235 m / 25 g)
YARN AMOUNTS:
250 (300, 400) g Tynn Alpakka
100 (125, 150) g Air
COLOR VERSION 1: Tynn Alpakka, Beige 184 and Air, Beige DL 119

COLOR VERSION 2: Tynn Alpakka, Gray-Blue Heather 187 and Air, Bluebell DL 114
COLOR VERSION 3: Tynn Alpakka, Yellow-Green 116 and Air, Green DL 106
NEEDLES: U.S. size 8 / 5 mm, circular 32 or 40 in / 80 or 100 cm; cable needle
CROCHET HOOK: U.S. size 7 / 4.5 mm
GAUGE: 14 sts in garter st, holding one strand each Tynn Alpakka and Air together = 4 in / 10 cm.
Adjust needle size to obtain correct gauge if necessary.

————————

This poncho features pretty cables and ties with pompoms. It is worked back and forth from side to side, holding one strand of each yarn together. The bell shape is produced with short rows.

PONCHO

Holding one strand each of Tynn Alpakka and Air together, CO 115 (121, 127) sts and work as follows:
Row 1: Work 30 sts following Chart 1, k54 (60, 66) sts in garter st (= knit all rows), 31 sts following Chart 2. Turn.

Row 2 and all WS rows: Work as est with garter st over garter st, Chart 1 over Chart 1, and Chart 2 over Chart 2.

Row 3: Work Chart 1, k18 (20, 22) in garter st; turn and work back.

NOTE: Each time you turn on the short rows, tighten yarn.

Row 5: Work Chart 1, k36 (40, 44) in garter st; turn and work back.

Row 7: Work Chart 1, k54 (60, 66) in garter st; turn and work back.

Row 9: Work Chart 1, k54 (60, 66) in garter st, 31 sts of Chart 2; turn and work back.

Row 11: Work Chart 1, k54 (60, 66) in garter st, 31 sts of Chart 2; turn and work back.

Row 13: Work Chart 1, k18 (20, 22) in garter st; turn and work back.

Row 15: Work Chart 1, k54 (60, 66) in garter st; turn and work back.

Row 17: Work Chart 1, k36 (40, 44) in garter st; turn and work back.

Row 19: Work Chart 1, k54 (60, 66) in garter st; turn and work back.

Row 21: Work Chart 1, k54 (60, 66) in garter st, 31 sts of Chart 2; turn and work back.

Row 23: Work Chart 1, k54 (60, 66) in garter st, 18 sts of Chart 2; turn and work back.

Row 25: Work Chart 1, k18 (20, 22) in garter st; turn and work back.

Row 27: Work Chart 1, k36 (40, 44) in garter st; turn and work back.

Row 29: Work Chart 1, k54 (60, 66) in garter st; turn and work back.

Row 31: Work Chart 1, k54 (60, 66) in garter st, 23 sts of Chart 2; turn and work back.

Rep Rows 1–32 until the longest part of the piece (lower edge) measures approx. 78¾ (78¾, 83½) in 200 (200, 212) cm. End after a complete repeat in length of Charts 1 and 2. BO.

FINISHING

Join the cast-on and bound-off edges either by sewing or knitting (3-needle BO) seams.

Cord: Holding one strand each Tynn Alpakka and Air together, use crochet hook to make a cord of chain sts about 39½ in / 100 cm long. Turn and work back with 1 sl st into each ch. Draw the cord through the eyelet row at the neck.

Pompoms: Make two fluffy pompoms each about 2 in / 5 cm in diameter—use both yarns together. Securely sew a pompom to each end of the cord.

Chart 1

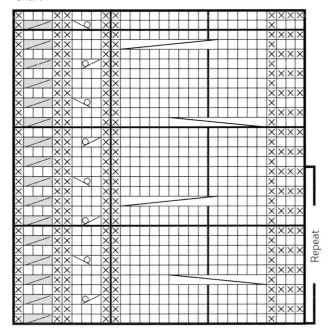

Repeat

Chart 2

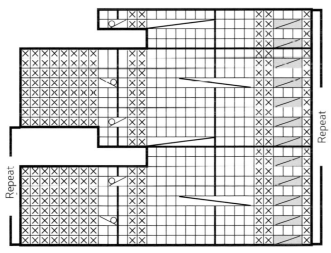

Repeat

Repeat

☐	Knit on RS, purl on WS
☒	Purl on RS, knit on WS
	K2tog, yo (eyelet)
	Yo, ssk
	Knit the 3rd st on left needle, knit sts 1 and 2, sl all sts to right needle
	Sl 4 sts to cn and hold in front of work, k4, k4 from cn
	Sl 4 sts to cn and hold in back of work, k4, k4 from cn
	Sl 5 sts to cn and hold in front of work, k5, k5 from cn
	Sl 5 sts to cn and hold in back of work, k5, k5 from cn

HONEYCOMB BRIOCHE PONCHO

Design: Denise Samson

SIZE
One size

FINISHED MEASUREMENTS
Each piece: 22 x 30 in / 56 x 76 cm

MATERIALS

YARN: CYCA #1 (fingering) Alpakka Silke from Sandnes Garn (70% alpaca, 30% mulberry silk; 218 yd/199 m / 50 g)
AND CYCA #4 (worsted/afghan/Aran) Silk Mohair from Sandnes Garn (60% mohair, 25% silk, 15% wool; 306 yd/280 m / 50 g)

YARN AMOUNTS:
200 g Alpakka Silke, Green 7741
150 g Silk Mohair, Green 7572

NEEDLES: U.S. size 10 / 6 mm, circular 32 in / 80 cm

GAUGE: 11 sts in pattern = 4 in / 10 cm.
Adjust needle size to obtain correct gauge if necessary.

I knitted this poncho with two yarns held together. The lustrous Alpakka Silke enhances the honey-comb brioche with a luxurious effect. The poncho's quite light even though it's knitted with two yarns, and the brioche makes it look like doubled stitches. The poncho is worked back and forth.

HONEYCOMB BRIOCHE

Row 1 (WS): K1, (yo, sl 1 purlwise, k1) to last 2 sts and end with k2.
Row 2: K1, (k2, sl 1 purlwise) to last st and end k1.
Row 3: K1, (knit the yarnover and next st tog, yo, sl 1 purlwise) to last st and end k1.
Row 4: K2, (sl 1 purlwise, k2) across.
Row 5: K1, (yo, sl 1 purlwise, knit the yarnover and next st tog) to last st and end k1.
Rep Rows 2–5.

Holding one strand of each yarn together, CO 92 sts. Work in Honeycomb Brioche until piece measures approx. 22 in / 56 cm. BO loosely (1 yo and 1 knit st are bound off together as one st).

Make the second piece the same way.

FINISHING
Join the short side of the first piece to the long side of the second piece. Join the short side of the second piece to the long side of the first piece. See sketch on page 6.

NET CROCHETED PONCHO
WITH PICOTS

NET CROCHETED PONCHO
WITH PICOTS

Design: Denise Samson

SIZE
One size

FINISHED MEASUREMENTS
EACH PIECE: 22 x 33 in / 56 x 84 cm
TOTAL LENGTH AFTER FINISHING: 34¼ in / 87 cm

MATERIALS
YARN: CYCA #1 (light fingering) Silk Blend from Manos del Uruguay (70% Merino wool, 30% silk; 490 yd/448 m / 100 g)
YARN AMOUNTS:
250 g Stellar 7292
CROCHET HOOK: U.S. size C-2 / 2.5 mm

This crocheted poncho is made in two matching pieces that are then sewn together. It is light and lofty and the pattern is the same on both sides. The variegated-color yarn means that the poncho can be worn with many different colors. The pattern is a multiple of 4 stitches.

Picot: Ch 3, work 1 sc in the st just made.

PONCHO
Ch 144.

Row 1: Work 1 dc in the 8th ch from hook, ch 3, work 1 sc in dc just made = 1 picot, *ch 5, skip 3 sts, work 1 dc, 1 picot*. Rep * to * across, ending with ch 5, 1 dc in the 3rd ch of ch loop.
Row 2: *Ch 5, 1 dc in 3rd st of ch loop, 1 picot*. Rep * to *, ending with ch 5, 1 dc in 3rd st of ch loop.
Rep Row 2 until piece measures 33 in / 84 cm. Make another piece the same way.

FINISHING
Pin out the pieces to finished measurements and and carefully steam press under a damp pressing cloth.
Join the short side of the first piece to the long side of the second piece. Join long side of first piece to short side of second piece, leaving an opening for the head and a point at both front and back. See sketch on page 6.

Edging: Work 5 rnds single crochet all around poncho edges. Weave in all ends neatly on WS.

LARGE CIRCULAR NECK/ HEART WARMER

Design: Denise Samson

This lovely soft cowl is knitted with my favorite yarn, Hexa. The cowl is large enough that you can also wear it as a heart-warmer—or soul-warmer, as it's sometimes called. It is knitted in the round.

SIZES

S/M (L/XL)

FINISHED MEASUREMENTS

CHEST: 39½ (44) in / 100 (112) cm
LENGTH: 17 in / 43 cm

MATERIALS

YARN: CYCA #5 (bulky) Hexa from Du Store Alpakka (100% Merino wool; 109 yd/100 m / 50 g)
YARN AMOUNTS:
250 (300) g Gray-Blue 933
NEEDLES: U.S. sizes 10 / 6 mm, 24 or 32 in / 60 or 80 cm circular
CROCHET HOOK: U.S. size H-8 / 5 mm
GAUGE: 16 sts in pattern = 4 in / 10 cm.
Adjust needle size to obtain correct gauge if necessary.

COWL

CO 160 (180) sts. Join, being careful not to twist cast-on sts; pm for beg of rnd. Work around in pattern as follows:

Rnds 1–2: *K2, sl 2 purlwise wyf*; rep * to * around.
Rnds 3–4: Knit.
Rnds 5–6: *Sl 2 purlwise wyf, k2*; rep * to * around.
Rnds 7–8: Knit.

Rep Rnds 1–8 until piece measures 17 in / 43 cm. End with Rnds 1–2. BO loosely. Weave in all ends neatly on WS.

EDGING

With crochet hook:
Rnd 1: Work 1 sc in each st.
Rnd 2: Work 1 crab st in each sc around (crab st = sc worked from left to right). End with 1 sl st to 1st sc.

FINISHING TIP
If you want the edge to roll, use crab stitch. You can also work the edging only around one edge, as shown in this photo.

RIBBED PONCHO

Design: Kari Hestnes

SIZES
S/M (L/XL)

FINISHED MEASUREMENTS
25½ x 33 (28¼ x 35) in / 65 x 84 (72 x 89) cm

MATERIALS
GARN: CYCA #1 (fingering) Tynn Alpakka from Du Store Alpakka (100% alpaca; 183 yd/167 m / 50 g)
YARN AMOUNTS:
550 (600) g Green 185
NEEDLES: U.S. size 6 / 4 mm, short and long circulars
GAUGE: 19 sts in k4, p3 ribbing holding two strands together = 4 in / 10 cm.
Knit a swatch and measure the gauge after carefully steam pressing.
Adjust needle size to obtain correct gauge if necessary.

A classic poncho with tassels as the only embellishment. The ribbed poncho is made with two pieces that are sewn together. It is worked back and forth.

PONCHO

Holding two strands of yarn together, CO 123 (137) sts. Work back and forth in k4, p3 ribbing.
NOTE: The 1st row = WS and begins and ends with p4.
Work in ribbing until piece measures approx. 33 (35) in / 84 (89) cm. BO in ribbing so the edge will be smooth and resist rolling. Make another piece the same way.

FINISHING
Pin out pieces to finished measurements with WS facing up. Cover with a damp pressing cloth and gently steam press. Join one short side of the first piece to one long side of the second piece. Join the other short side of the first piece to the other long side of the second piece, leaving a V-neck opening for the head at both front and back. See sketch on page 7.
Twist 4 cords of doubled yarn, each about 2 in / 5 cm long. Make 4 tassels as shown in the drawing below and sew one tassel to each cord. The tassels should be about 2¾ in / 7 cm long. Sew the cords with their attached tassels to the poncho.

CROCHETED SHAWL IN LACE FAN PATTERN

Design: Denise Samson

SIZE
One size

FINISHED MEASUREMENTS INCLUDING EDGING
Approx. 22¾ x 61½ in / 58 x 156 cm

MATERIALS
YARN: CYCA #1 (light fingering) Silk Blend Fino from Manos del Uruguay (70% Merino wool, 30% silk; 490 yd/448 m/100 g)
YARN AMOUNTS:
250 g Jewel 6881
CROCHET HOOK: U.S. size C-2 / 2.5 mm

I used the gorgeous Silk Blend Fino for this shawl—and for the one shown on page 92, but with a different color combination. You can wear this as a scarf or shawl over a coat or fine summer dress. It's worked with an open fan stitch, across a multiple of 10 + 7 sts. This produces a smooth and harmonious pattern that emphasizes the multi-color yarn.

Open Fan: 1 tr, (ch 1, 1 tr) 4 times.

SHAWL
Ch 147.

Row 1: Work 1 sc in 2nd ch from hook *ch 1, skip 4 ch, work 1 open fan in the next ch, ch 1, skip 4 ch, 1 sc in next ch*. Rep * to * until 5 sts rem and end with ch 1, skip 4 ch, work (1 tr, ch 2, 1 tr, ch 2, 1 tr) in last ch; turn.

Row 2: Ch 1, 1 sc in first tr, *ch 3, skip next ch loop, 1 dc in next ch**, ch 2, skip next (tr, sc, tr) and work 1 dc in ch loop of next fan, ch 3, 1 sc in the 3rd tr of fan*. Rep * to * ending row at **, ch 1, 1 tr in last sc; turn.

Row 3: Ch 6 (= 1 tr + ch 1), skip first tr, work (1 tr, ch 2, 1 tr) in next ch loop, ch 1, skip ch loop, 1 sc in next sc, *ch 1, skip next ch loop, work 1 open fan in next ch loop, ch 1, skip next ch loop, 1 sc in next sc*. Rep* to *; turn.

Row 4: Ch 6 (= 1 tr + ch 1), skip first tr, work 1 dc in next ch loop, ch 3, 1 sc in center tr of fan, *ch 3, skip next ch loop, 1 dc in next ch loop, ch 2, skip next (tr, sc, tr) and work 1 dc in first ch loop of next fan, ch 3, 1 sc in the center tr of fan*. Rep * to *, ending with 1 sc in the 4th of the 6 ch.

Row 5: Ch 1, *1 sc in next sc, ch 1, skip next ch loop, 1 open fan in next ch loop, ch 1, skip next ch loop*. Rep * to * to last sc and ch loop. Work 1 sc in last

sc, ch 1, skip next ch loop, work (1 tr, ch 2, 1 tr, ch 2, 1 tr) in turning st; turn.

Rep Rows 2–5 until piece measures 57½ in / 146 cm. End with a Row 2 after the last Row 5.

EDGING

Rnd 1: Work sc all around the shawl.

Rnds 2–3: Work 1 dc in each sc around.

NOTE: At each corner, work 2 dc into corner st to round edge. Join each rnd with 1 sl st into 1st st of rnd.

Rnd 4: Work *ch 4, 1 tr in same st, skip 2 dc, 1 sl st into next st*. Rep * to * around.

FINISHING

Pin out shawl to finished measurements and carefully steam press under a damp pressing cloth. Weave in all ends neatly on WS.

PONCHO WITH RAGLAN CABLES

Design: Hrönn Jónsdóttir

SIZES
XS/S (M/L, XL/XXL)

FINISHED MEASUREMENTS
CIRCUMFERENCE: approx. 55¼ (60¾, 67) in / 140 (154, 170) cm
TOTAL LENGTH: approx. 28¼ (29½, 31½) in / 72 (75, 80) cm

MATERIALS
YARN: CYCA #1 (fingering) Tynn Alpakka from Du Store Alpakka (100% alpaca; 183 yd/167 m / 50 g)
AND CYCA #1 (fingering) Air from Du Store Alpakka (78% Suri alpaca, 22% nylon; 257 yd/235 m / 25 g)
YARN AMOUNTS:
350 (400, 450) g Tynn Alpakka, Slate Gray 128
250 (300, 350) g Air, Coal DL111

NEEDLES: U.S. sizes 2½ and 7 / 3 and 4.5 mm, short circulars; U.S. size 7 / 4.5 mm, 40 in / 100 cm circular; cable needle
GAUGE: 20 sts in St st with larger needle and holding one strand each Tynn Alpakka and Air together = 4 in / 10 cm.
Adjust needle sizes to obtain correct gauge if necessary.

This poncho is knitted with two yarns, Tynn Alpakka (fine alpaca) and Air, which combine for a light and sheer garment. The beautiful details—a cable along the raglan shaping line, the neck and puffed sleeves—make this a fresh, modern poncho. It's worked both back and forth and in the round.

FRONT
With larger circular and one strand of each yarn held together, CO 88 (100, 110) sts. Work back

82

and forth in garter st (knit all rows) until piece measures 2½ (2¾, 2¾) in / 6 (7, 7) cm.
NOTE: On the last row, increase evenly spaced across to 98 (110, 122) sts. Work the next row as follows:
Work 9 sts of Chart 1, work in St st until 9 sts rem, work Chart 2. Continue as est until piece measures 14¼ (14½, 15½) in / 36 (37, 39) cm. Set front aside and make the back.

BACK

With larger circular and one strand of each yarn held together, CO 88 (100, 110) sts. Work back and forth in garter st (knit all rows) until piece measures 2½ (2¾, 2¾) in / 6 (7, 7) cm.
NOTE: On the last row, increase evenly spaced across to 98 (110, 122) sts.

Change to St st, and, *at the same time*, increase at each side as follows (increase rows are spaced about ³⁄₈ in / 1 cm apart):
Size XS/S: CO 7 new sts at each side 5 times and 6 new sts 2 times = 192 sts.
Size M/L: CO 7 new sts at each side 7 times = 208 sts.
Size XL/XXL: CO 6 new sts at each side 8 times and 5 new sts once = 228 sts.

All sizes: Continue, increasing 1 st at each side every 1¼ in / 3 cm (inc with k1f&b in first and last sts of row) a total of 3 times = 198 (214, 234) sts. Continue without further shaping until back is 10¾ (11, 11¾) in / 27 (28, 30) cm. Dec 1 st at each side every 1¼ in / 3 cm a total of 3 times = 192 (208, 228) sts.
Work in St st until back measures 14¼ (14½, 15½) in / 36 (37, 39) cm. CO 3 new sts at the end of the next 2 rows = 198 (214, 234) sts.

Slip the front sts onto the needle with the sts for the back = 296 (324, 356) sts. Join to knit in the round. Pm at each side of the front—one to indicate beg of rnd = the left side, where front begins, and the other (use a different color marker at side) at the opposite side of the garment. Dec 1 st at each side of each marker about every ⁵⁄₈ in / 1.5 cm a total of 26 (27, 29) times as follows: Work Chart 1 as before, k2tog, knit until 11 sts before next marker, ssk, work Chart 2 to next marker, slm,

k2tog, knit until 2 sts before next marker, ssk = 4 sts decreased.
NOTE: *At the same time* as the 24th (25th, 27th) decrease rnd, BO the center 32 (42, 50) sts on the front for the neck and then work back and forth. Decrease at neck edge on every other row by binding off 3-2 sts.
NOTE: The last 2 decreases at the side markers on the front are made by working k2tog after the first marker and ssk before the next marker. After completing all the decreases, 150 (164, 180) sts rem. Work the next row as follows:
K2tog 25 (27, 30) times, k50 (56, 60), k2tog 25 (27, 30) times = 100 (110, 120) sts rem.
Now BO 25 (27, 30) sts at the beg of the next 2 rows = 50 (56, 60) sts rem at the center. Leave the sts on the needle.

FINISHING

Pick up and knit 48 (58, 66) sts along the neck on the front and place them on the same needle as the 50 (56, 60) center sts of back = 98 (114, 126) sts total. Work around in garter st (alternate 1 purl rnd, 1 knit rnd). *At the same time*, decrease evenly spaced around the 1st rnd to 96 (102, 106) sts. Continue around in garter st until neckband is 10¼ (10¾, 11) in / 26 (27, 28) cm or desired length. BO. Seam the 2½ (2¾, 2¾) in / 6 (7, 7) cm in garter st at each side of the bottom edge. Baste a thread through the 25 (27, 30) sts at each side of the neck and tighten well.
With smaller circular, pick up and knit 86 (90, 94) sts along the side opening of the back and knit 3 rows back and forth. BO and work an edging the same way along the opening at the opposite side.

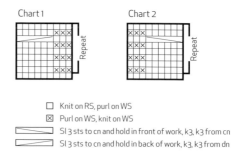

Chart 1   Chart 2

☐ Knit on RS, purl on WS
⊠ Purl on WS, knit on WS
▱ Sl 3 sts to cn and hold in front of work, k3, k3 from cn
▱ Sl 3 sts to cn and hold in back of work, k3, k3 from dn

HOODED PONCHO

Design: Denise Samson

SIZE
One size

FINISHED MEASUREMENTS
Excluding ribbed band without cables: 19¾ x 59 in / 50 x 150 cm

MATERIALS
YARN: CYCA #4 (worsted/afghan/Aran) Alpakka Tweed from Du Store Alpakka (50% alpaca, 50% Merino wool; 87 yd/80 m / 50 g)
YARN AMOUNTS:
800 g Blue 104
NEEDLES: U.S. sizes 7 and 8 / 4.5 and 5 mm, long circulars; 2 dpn U.S. size 7 / 4.5 mm for I-cord; cable needle
CROCHET HOOK: U.S. size H-8 / 5 mm for seaming
GAUGE: 17 sts in St st with larger needles = 4 in / 10 cm. Adjust needle sizes to obtain correct gauge if necessary.

This tweed yarn is so fantastically soft to knit with. The cable design at center front and the ribbing along the bottom edge really bring out the yarn's best qualities. A nice hood for cold days makes this poncho a sporty garment. It's worked back and forth except for the ribbed lower edge, which is worked in the round.

EDGE STITCHES
Always slip the first st purlwise with yarn in front; knit last st through back loop.

PONCHO
With larger circular, CO 76 sts and work back and forth in St st until piece measures 59 in / 150 cm. BO.

TRELLIS CABLE PANEL
With larger needles, CO 40 sts and work in cable pattern following the chart on page 88. BO when piece measures 19¾ in / 50 cm.

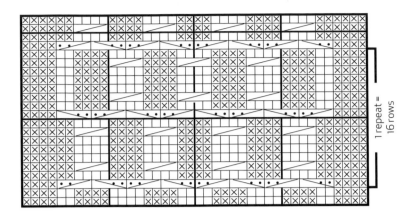

1 repeat = 16 rows

☐ Knit on RS, purl on WS

☒ Purl on RS, knit on WS

▱ Sl 2 sts to cn and hold in back of work, k2, k2 from cn

▱ Sl 2 purl sts to cn and hold in back of work, k2, p2 from cn

▱ Sl 2 knit sts to cn and hold in front of work, p2, k2 from cn

FINISHING

Weave in all ends neatly on WS.
With WS facing up, pin out large rectangular piece to finished measurements and carefully steam press under a damp pressing cloth. Fold the piece in two equal-sized parts—29½ in / 75 cm for each section—and place one side of the cable panel along one side of the rectangle piece with WS facing WS. Crochet together with 1 sl st into the outermost stitch loop of each part, or seam with whip stitch. Seam the other side to match. See sketch on page 7.

LOWER EDGE

Place a locking ring stitch marker at each corner and, with smaller circular, begin picking up and knitting sts along the cable panel. Pick up 4 sts for every 5 sts. Pick up and knit 118 sts to the first marker, pick up and knit 1 corner st, 232 sts to the next marker, 1 corner st, 82 sts to cable panel. Work in k4, p4 ribbing until 3 sts before marker, p2, k1 = corner st (corner sts are always knitted). P2, (k4, p4) until 3 sts before next marker, p2, k1 (corner st). P2 (k4, p4) to cable. Continue as est with knit over knit and purl over purl and, *at the same time,* increase 1 st on each side of each marker (purling the new sts) on every other rnd until the ribbing is 2 in / 5 cm long. BO in ribbing.

HOOD

With smaller circular, pick up and knit 96 sts around the neck, beginning at about the center of the cable panel. Pick up and knit 4 sts for every 5 sts. Work in St st until hood measures 12¾ in / 32 cm. Turn hood inside out, divide sts 48-48 and bind off with 3-needle bind-off.

CASING AROUND HOOD

With smaller circular, pick up and knit 120 sts (4 sts for every 5). Knit 1 row = WS. Work 5 rows in St st and BO on WS.

I-CORD

With smaller dpn, CO 3 sts and k3. *Do not turn; slide sts back to tip of needle and k3; rep from * until cord is about 55 in / 140 cm long. Cut yarn and draw end through rem sts. Lay the cord in the hood casing and then sew down the casing with whip stitch on WS, working through the cast-on sts.

TASSELS (MAKE 3)

Using a heavy paper template, or something else that measures about 4 in / 10 cm around, twist the yarn about 20 times around the template and wrap securely at the top. Remove the yarn from the template and twist yarn around the tassel about ¾–1¼ in / 2–3 cm from the top. Fasten off securely. Trim the lower edges of the tassel to even up. Sew one tassel to the tip of the hood and one at each end of the hood cord.

SHORT HOODED PONCHO

Design: Turid Stapnes

SIZE
One size

FINISHED MEASUREMENTS
TOTAL LENGTH: 17¾ in / 45 cm

MATERIALS
YARN: CYCA #5 (bulky) Alpaca Maya from Viking of Norway (82% alpaca, 13% Merino wool, 5% nylon; 175 yd/160 m / 50 g)
YARN AMOUNTS:
200 g Blue 927
NOTIONS: 3 large decorative buttons
NEEDLES: U.S. sizes 10 and 10½ or 11 / 6 and 7 mm, circulars
GAUGE: 12 sts in St st with larger needles = 4 in / 10 cm. Adjust needle sizes to obtain correct gauge if necessary.

————————

A lovely short poncho with a hood and buttoned at the front. It'll look just as good over a sweater as over a warm coat. It's worked back and forth with short rows to fashion a pretty bell shape.

PONCHO
With larger needles, CO 54 sts and work back and forth in k3, p3 ribbing for approx. 1¼ in / 3 cm. Now work in garter st and short rows as follows: *[K54; turn and k54. K45 sts; turn and k45. K36 sts; turn and k36. K27; turn and k27. K18; turn and k18. K9; turn and k9] 8 times. Knit 6 ridges (= 12 rows) over all the sts*. Rep * to * a total of 4 times. After the last turn, finish with k3, p3 ribbing for about 1¼ in / 3 cm. BO in ribbing.

HOOD AND NECKBAND
With smaller circular, beginning at ribbed edge, pick up and knit 69 sts around the neck. Work in k3, p3 ribbing for about 2 in / 5 cm. Now work in k3, p3 ribbing over the first 6 sts and last 6 sts and in St st over the rem 57 sts. Pm around the st at center back.

On the next, RS, row, inc 1 st in each of the 13 knit sts at center back = 82 sts total. Continue working back and forth. When the hood measures approx. 10¼ in / 26 cm (as measured from the increased sts), dec 1 st at each side of the center back marker on every other row 3 times = 76 sts rem. Divide the hood sts 38-38 at center back and, with WS facing, use Kitchener st or three-needle bind-off to join.

FINISHING
Overlap the front edges and fasten with 3 decorative buttons so the poncho closes at center front (see photo on facing page).

CROCHETED SHAWL IN SHELL NET PATTERN

Design: Denise Samson

The combination of the softest Merino wool and the finest silk produces a wonderful luster and a yarn that is lovely to crochet with in a fun pattern. You can wear this large shawl with everything and you can decide how big to make it. The pattern is a multiple of 12 sts + 1 + 2 sts for the foundation chain.

SIZE
One size

FINISHED MEASUREMENTS
INCLUDING EDGINGS: 18¼ x 61½ in / 46 x 156 cm

MATERIALS
YARN: CYCA #1 (light fingering) Silk Blend Fino from Manos del Uruguay (70% Merino wool, 30% silk; 490 yd/448 m/100 g)
YARN AMOUNTS:
250 g Autumn SB3106
CROCHET HOOK: U.S. size C-2 / 2.5 mm

SHAWL
Ch 123.

Row 1: Work 2 dc in 3rd ch from hook, *skip 2 ch, 1 sc in next ch, ch 5, skip 5 ch, 1 sc in next ch, skip 2 ch, 5 dc in next ch*. Rep * to * across, ending with 3 dc in last ch; turn.
Row 2: Ch 1, 1 sc in next dc, *ch 5, 1 sc in next ch loop, ch 5, 1 sc in 3rd of the 5 dc*. Rep * to * across, ending with 1 sc in the 2nd ch of ch 2; turn.

Row 3: *Ch 5, 1 sc in next ch loop, 5 dc in next sc, 1 sc in next ch loop*. Rep * to * across, ending with ch 2 and 1 dc in last sc; turn.

Row 4: Ch 1, 1 sc in next dc, *ch 5, 1 sc in the 3rd of 5 dc, ch 5, 1 sc in next ch loop*. Rep * to * across; turn.

Row 5: Ch 3 (= 1st dc), 2 dc in next sc, *1 sc in next ch loop, ch 5, 1 sc in next ch loop, 5 dc in next sc*. Rep * to * across, ending with 3 dc in last sc; turn.
Rep Rows 2–5 until piece measures 57½ in / 146 cm.

EDGING

Rnd 1: Work 1 rnd sc all around shawl.

Rnds 2–6: Work 1 dc in each sc around. At each corner, work 2 dc into same st to round the edges. End each rnd with 1 sl st into 1st st.

Rnd 7: Work (5 dc in the same st, skip 2 dc) around and end with 1 sl st into 1st st. Cut yarn and draw end through last st to fasten off.

FINISHING

Pin out shawl to finished measurements and carefully steam press under a damp pressing cloth. Weave in all ends neatly on WS.

AUTUMN PONCHO

Design: Denise Samson

GAUGE: 15 sts in pattern holding one strand each Sterk and Tynn Alpakka together = 4 in / 10 cm.
Adjust needle size to obtain correct gauge if necessary.

_____

A warm and wonderful poncho knitted with one strand of each yarn held together. The pattern is made by slipping a stitch with the yarn in back of the work. The poncho is worked in the round. The headband is worked back and forth, with the yarn strand held alternately in front of and in back of the piece.

SIZES
S/M (L/XL)

FINISHED MEASUREMENTS
TOTAL LENGTH: 29½ (30¾) in / 75 (78) cm

MATERIALS
YARN: CYCA #3 (DK/light worsted) Sterk from Du Store Alpakka (40% Merino wool, 40% alpaca, 20% nylon; 150 yd/137 m / 50 g)
AND
CYCA #1 (fingering) Tynn Alpakka from Du Store Alpakka (100% alpaca; 183 yd/167 m / 50 g)
YARN AMOUNTS:
300 (350) g Sterk, Terracotta 836
250 (300) g Tynn Alpakka, Terracotta 143
NEEDLES: U.S. size 10 / 6 mm, short and long circulars and set of 5 dpn

SLIP STITCH PATTERN IN THE ROUND
Rnd 1: (Sl 1 knitwise wyb, p1) around.
Rnd 2: (Sl 1 knitwise wyb, p1) around.
Rnd 3: Knit around.
Rnd 4: Purl around.

PONCHO

With long circular and holding one strand of each yarn together, CO 210 (240) sts. Join, being careful not to twist cast-on row; pm for beg of rnd. Work around in garter st (alternating knit and purl rnds) for 1¼ in / 3 cm. Make sure knitting is not twisted on the needle. Pm at the center of the front and back = 105 (120) sts between markers. Work in the Slip Stitch pattern above until piece measures 2¾ in / 7 cm from cast-on row. Now begin shaping as follows: after the first marker, k2tog 4 times, work until 8 sts before next marker, k2tog 8 times, work until 8 sts before next marker and k2tog 4 times = 16 sts decreased = 194 (224) sts rem.
NOTE: Always decrease on a Rnd 3 of pattern. Decrease the same way every 2¾ in / 7 cm a total of 7 (8) times = 98 (112) sts rem. Work 1 rnd in pattern without decreasing. On the next rnd (Rnd 3) in pattern, decrease as follows: *Sl 1 knitwise, p1, k2tog*; rep * to * around. End S/M with k2 = 74 (84) sts rem. Work in pattern until piece measures 29¼ (30¼) in / 74 (77) cm. Make 1 garter ridge (= knit 1 rnd, purl 1 rnd) and then BO.

SLEEVES

Lay the poncho flat and find the center at each side and pm. With dpn and holding both yarns together, at right side of poncho, pick up and knit 15 (16) sts on each side of marker = 30 (32) sts. Divide sts onto dpn; join. Work in pattern for 3¼ in / 8 cm. BO. Make the sleeve for the left side the same way.

HEADBAND

Design: Denise Samson

SIZES
S/M (L/XL)

FINISHED MEASUREMENTS
Circumference: 20½ (22) in / 52 (56) cm

MATERIALS
YARN: CYCA #3 (DK/light worsted) Sterk from Du Store Alpakka (40% Merino wool, 40% alpaca, 20% nylon; 150 yd/137 m / 50 g)
AND
CYCA #1 (fingering) Tynn Alpakka from Du Store Alpakka (100% alpaca; 183 yd/167 m / 50 g)
YARN AMOUNTS:
Leftovers from poncho
NEEDLES: U.S. size 10 / 6 mm, short circular
GAUGE: 15 sts in pattern holding one strand each Sterk and Tynn Alpakka together = 4 in / 10 cm.
Adjust needle size to obtain correct gauge if necessary.

SLIP STITCH PATTERN WORKED BACK AND FORTH
Row 1: (Sl 1 knitwise wyb, p1) across.
Row 2: (K1, sl 1 knitwise wyf) across.
Row 3: Knit.
Row 4: Knit.

CO 62 (70) sts and work back and forth in Slip Stitch pattern above until piece measures 3¼ in / 8 cm. BO and seam the short ends together.

Small Strip: CO 10 sts and work back and forth in Slip Stitch pattern above until piece measures approx. 5½ in / 14 cm. BO. Wrap the strip around the headband at the seam and sew the cast-on edge to the bound-off edge.

CELTIC KNOT PONCHO

Design: Denise Samson

SIZE
One size

FINISHED MEASUREMENTS
TOTAL LENGTH, FRONT: 27½ in / 70 cm
Total length, excluding ribbed edging: approx. 20½ x
55¼ in / 52 x 140 cm

MATERIALS
YARN: CYCA #3 (DK/light worsted) Sterk from Du Store
Alpakka (40% Merino wool, 40% alpaca, 20% nylon; 150
yd/137 m / 50 g)
YARN AMOUNTS:
400 g Light Gray 822 OR Petroleum 813
NEEDLES: U.S. size 4 / 3.5 mm, very long circular and U.S.
size 6 / 4 mm, 24 in / 60 cm circular or straights; cable
needle
CROCHET HOOK: U.S. size D-3 / 3 mm

GAUGE: 21 sts in St st on larger needles = 4 in / 10 cm.
Adjust needle sizes to obtain correct gauge if necessary.
KNITTING TECHNIQUES: Stockinette (St st), charted
cable pattern
CROCHET TECHNIQUES: Single crochet (sc), slip st (sl
st), and crab stitch (single crochet worked from left to
right)

_____

My good friend Randi gave me the idea for this
poncho. She thought a poncho with a Celtic knot
pattern knitted down one shoulder would be
elegant—and she was right! The poncho is worked
back and forth except for the lower edging, which
is knitted in the round.

Edge Stitches: Always slip the first st purlwise
with yarn held in front and knit the last st through
the back loop.

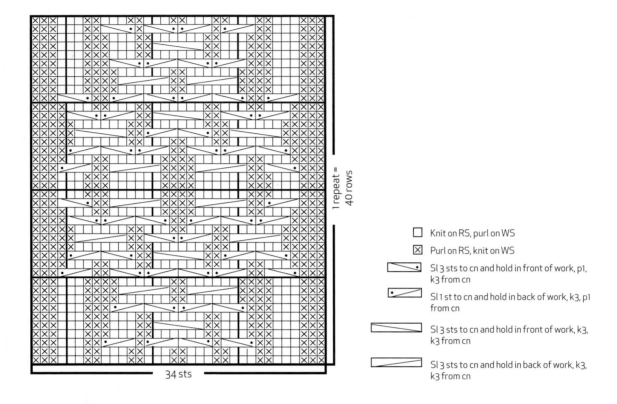

1 repeat = 40 rows

34 sts

☐ Knit on RS, purl on WS

☒ Purl on RS, knit on WS

Sl 3 sts to cn and hold in front of work, p1, k3 from cn

Sl 1 st to cn and hold in back of work, k3, p1 from cn

Sl 3 sts to cn and hold in front of work, k3, k3 from cn

Sl 3 sts to cn and hold in back of work, k3, k3 from cn

PONCHO

With larger needles, CO 100 sts. Work back and forth in St st until piece is approx. 55¼ in / 140 cm long. BO.

CABLE PANEL

With larger needles, CO 34 sts and work back and forth in pattern following the chart on page 100. Work the chart repeat a total of 3 times = approx. 17¾ in / 45 cm. End with Rows 1 and 2 on the chart and then BO.

FINISHING

Carefully steam press poncho pieces under a damp pressing cloth, or lay them flat between two damp towels. Leave until completely dry.

Fold the stockinette section into two halves = 27½ in / 70 cm each half. Place the cable panel and one long side of the poncho together with WS facing WS. Crochet the pieces together with

slip st in the outermost stitch loop of each piece. Join the other side of the panel to the poncho the same way. See the sketch on page 7.

LOWER EDGE

With smaller circular, and beginning at the cable panel, pick up and knit 610 sts around the poncho. Begin with p2, k3 to match the stitches in the cable panel. The stitch count is a multiple of 5. Pm at each corner (the point at front and back). Mark the 3 corner sts which are always knitted. Inc 1 st before and after these 3 marked sts on every other rnd. Always knit the new sts. Work rem sts as p2, k3 ribbing. When edging is 1½ in / 4 cm wide, BO with knit over knit and purl over purl.

NECKBAND

Work 1 rnd of sc around neckline and then 1 rnd crab st. Cut yarn and weave in all ends neatly on WS.

DENISE PONCHO

Design: Denise Samson

SIZES
S/M (L/XL)

FINISHED MEASUREMENTS
Total length, excluding crocheted edging, **BOTH SIZES:**
approx. 24½ in / 62 cm
Total length with crocheted edging: approx. 25½ 65 cm

MATERIALS
YARN: CYCA #2 (sport/baby) Baby Silk from Du Store Alpakka (80% baby alpaca, 20% mulberry silk; 145 yd/133 m / 50 g)
YARN AMOUNTS:
350 (400) g Beige 324
100 (100) g Natural White 301
150 (150) g Petroleum 345
1 spool Du Store Alpakka Bling effect thread, Beige (100% polyester, 382 yd/346 m / 50 g)

NEEDLES: U.S. size 4 / 3.5: circulars 24, 32, and 60 in / 60, 80, and 150 cm
CROCHET HOOK: U.S. size D-3 / 3 mm
GAUGE: 24 sts in St st = 4 in / 10 cm.
Adjust needle size to obtain correct gauge if necessary.

I previously used this pattern for the Denise sweater, knitted in gray, red, and natural white. I think the pattern also works well for a poncho in these colors. To spark up the star motifs, I knitted a strand of bling thread with the alpaca/silk yarn.

KNITTING TIP!
Change to a longer circular when the stitches begin to be too tightly packed. If you want to adjust the length of the poncho, you can add or subtract length in the single-color section.

The poncho is worked in the round from the top down.

Increase: M1 = lift strand between two sts and knit into back loop.

PONCHO

SIZE S/M
With short circular and Petroleum, CO 98 sts. Join, being careful not to twist cast-on row; pm for beg of rnd. Work around in pattern following Chart 1. Inc on the rnds as indicated by arrows.
First inc rnd: K1, M1, (k2, M1) 48 times, k1 = 147 sts. The increases are worked with Beige so you will have (2 Beige, 1 White) around.

Second inc rnd: K3, (M1, k3) 48 times = 196 sts. Now there are (2 Beige and 2 White) sts around.

Now work Chart 2, increasing at arrows as follows:
First inc rnd, Chart 2: (K2, M1, k3, M1) 33 times, (k3, M1, k4, M1) 4 times, k3 = 270 sts. Continue following Chart 2, holding a strand Beige 324 with 1 strand Bling for the Beige. At the next inc arrow, work:
Second inc rnd, Chart 2: K8, M1, (k6, M1) 20 times, k15, M1, (k6, M1) 20 times, k7 = 312 sts.

Continue on to Chart 3, increasing at the first arrow:
K9, M1, (k14, M1) 21 times, k9 = 334 sts.
At the next arrow, increase as K2, M1, (k10, M1) 33 times, k2 = 368 sts.

Pm at each side with 184 sts between the markers. M1 at each side of each marker every ¾ in / 2 cm (= inc on every 6th rnd) a total of 20 times = 80 new sts = 448 sts total. When piece measures 22 in / 56 cm, divide into two sections with 224 sts in each. Work Chart 4 back and forth so you will have slits at the sides. After completing Chart 4, BO. Work the other half the same way.

SIZE L/ XL
With short circular and Petroleum, CO 124 sts. Join, being careful not to twist cast-on row; pm for beg of rnd. Work around in pattern following Chart 1. Inc on the rnds as indicated by arrows.
First inc rnd: K1, M1, (k2, M1) 61 times, k1 = 186 sts. The increases are worked with Beige so you will have (2 Beige, 1 White) around.
Second inc rnd: K2, M1, (k3, M1) 61 times, k1 = 248 sts. Now there are (2 Beige and 2 White) sts around.

Now work Chart 2, increasing at arrows as follows:
First inc rnd, Chart 2: K4, M1, (k5, M1) 48 times, k4 = 297 sts.
Continue following Chart 2, holding a strand Beige 324 with 1 strand Bling for the Beige. At the next inc arrow, work as follows:
Second inc rnd, Chart 2: K8, M1, (k7, M1) 19 times, k15, (k7, M1) 19 times, k8 = 336 sts.

Continue on to Chart 3, increasing at the first arrow:
K7, M1, (k14, M1) 23 times, k7 = 360 sts.
At the next arrow, increase as:

Chart 1

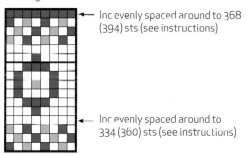

← Inc evenly spaced around to 196 (248) sts

← Inc evenly spaced around to 147 (186) sts

← Cast-on row 98 (124) sts

Chart 2

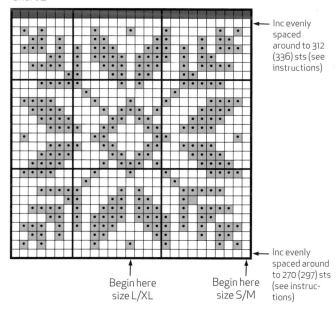

← Inc evenly spaced around to 312 (336) sts (see instructions)

← Inc evenly spaced around to 270 (297) sts (see instructions)

Begin here size L/XL

Begin here size S/M

K7, M1, (k10, M1) 16 times, k15, (k10, M1) 17 times, k8 = 394 sts.

Pm at each side with 197 sts between the markers. M1 at each side of each marker every ¾ in / 2 cm (= inc on every 6th rnd) a total of 20 times = 80 new sts = 474 sts total. When piece measures 22 in / 56 cm, divide into two sections with 237 sts in each. Work Chart 4 back and forth so you will have slits at the sides. On the first row of Chart 4, dec 1 st at the center = 236 sts rem. After completing Chart 4, BO. Work the other half the same way.

NECKBAND

Rnd 1: With Petroleum, work 1 rnd of sc around; end with 1 sl st to first sc.
Rnds 2–3: Work as for Rnd 1.
Rnd 4: *1 sc, skip 2 sts, work (2 dc, ch 2, 2 dc) in next st, skip 2 sts*. Rep * to * around. End with 1 sl st into 1st sc.
Cut yarn and bring end through last loop.

LOWER EDGE

With Petroleum and RS facing, crochet beginning at a split at one side. Work sc across to next split and then sc up split. Turn and sc back and up the split on opposite side. Turn, but when you come to the split on the other side, do not work up the edge of the split; turn and ch 1; continue with sc back to split on opposite side; turn with ch 1 and sc back. You should now have 5 rows of sc. End with *1 sc, skip 2 sts, work (2 dc, ch 2, 2 dc) in next st, skip 2 sts*. Rep * to * across. Sc up the last split.
Cut yarn and work the other side the same way.

Chart 3

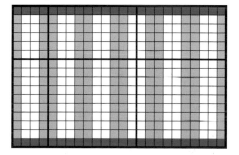

← Inc evenly spaced around to 368 (394) sts (see instructions)

← Inc evenly spaced around to 334 (360) sts (see instructions)

Chart 4

□ Natural White 301
▨ Beige 324
⊡ Beige 324 + Bling
▨ Petroleum 345
■ No stitch
◎ M1 inc

DENISE HAT

Design: Denise Samson

SIZE
Women's

MATERIALS
YARN: CYCA #2 (sport/baby) Baby Silk from Du Store Alpakka (80% baby alpaca, 20% mulberry silk; 145 yd/133 m / 50 g)

YARN AMOUNTS:
50 g Beige 324
50 g Natural White 301
50 g Petroleum 345
+ 1 spool Du Store Alpakka Bling effect thread, Beige (100% polyester, 382 yd/346 m / 50 g)
(you can use leftovers from the poncho)
NEEDLES: U.S. size 4 / 3.5: circular 16 in / 40 cm and set of 5 dpn
CROCHET HOOK: U.S. size D-3 / 3 mm
GAUGE: 24 sts in St st = 4 in / 10 cm.
Adjust needle size to obtain correct gauge if necessary.

With Petroleum and short circular, CO 136 sts. Join, being careful not to twist cast-on row; pm for beg of rnd. Work around in pattern following Chart 5 (don't forget to add the strand of Bling starting on first rnd with Beige).
NOTE: Inc 4 sts evenly spaced around last charted pattern row. When pattern is complete, 140 sts rem. Change to Beige + Bling yarn (1 strand of each held together) and shape crown as follows:
Rnd 1: (K12, ssk) around.
Rnd 2: Knit.
Rnd 3: (K11, ssk) around.
Rnd 4: Knit.
Rnd 5: (K10, ssk) around.
Continue decreasing every other rnd with 1 less st between decreases. Change to dpn when sts no longer fit around circular. On the last rnd, k2tog around. Cut yarn and draw end through rem 5 sts; tighten. Weave in all ends neatly on WS.

BRIM EDGING
Rnd 1: With Petroleum, work 1 sc in each st of cast-on row; end with 1 sl st to first sc.
Rnds 2–3: Work 1 sc in each sc around.
Rnd 4: *1 sc, skip 2 sts, work (2 dc, ch 2, 2 dc) in next st, skip 2 sts*. Rep * to * around. End with 1 sl st into 1st sc.
Cut yarn and bring end through last loop.

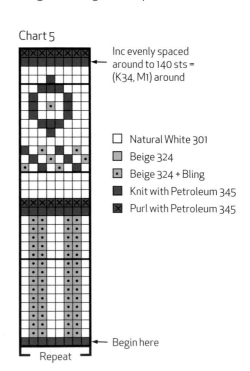

Chart 5

Inc evenly spaced around to 140 sts = (K34, M1) around

☐ Natural White 301
▨ Beige 324
⊡ Beige 324 + Bling
■ Knit with Petroleum 345
⊠ Purl with Petroleum 345

Begin here

Repeat

BASKET-WEAVE CABLE PONCHO

Design: Denise Samson

SIZES
S/M (L/XL)

FINISHED MEASUREMENTS
TOTAL LENGTH: 27½ (29½) in / 70 (75) cm

MATERIALS
YARN: CYCA #6 (super bulky) Pus from Du Store
Alpakka (70% alpaca, 17% acrylic, 13% nylon; 109 yd/100
m / 50 g)
YARN AMOUNTS:
400 (450) g Beige 4009
NEEDLES: U.S. size 13 / 9 mm, 32 in / 80 cm circular;
cable needle
GAUGE: 12 sts in texture pattern = 4 in / 10 cm.
Adjust needle size to obtain correct gauge if necessary.

This poncho is knitted in two pieces with one
section of basket-weave cables at the center
front. If you don't want cables across the center
front, just work the front as for the back and you'll
have cables only at the top and bottom (see photo
page 110).

NOTE: After completing Chart 2, always knit the
first and last sts on every row as edge sts.
**Decreases at the top of the front before the
pattern:** k2tog.
**Decreases at the top of the front after the pat-
tern:** ssk or k2tog tbl.
**Decreases at the top of the back inside 12 sts at
beginning of row 2:** ssk or k2tog tbl.
**Decreases at the top of the back inside 12 sts at
the end of the row:** k2tog.

FRONT
CO 130 (150) sts. Work back and forth in pattern
following chart 2 until piece measures 2½ in /
6 cm. On the last WS row, dec 26 (34) sts evenly

spaced across = 104 (116) sts rem. Continue in St st over 34 (40) sts, 36 sts of chart 1, St st over 34 (40) sts. On the next RS row, dec 1 st at each side inside each edge st as well as 1 st on each side of the cable = 4 sts decreased. Work 4 rows and then rep the dec row once more = 96 (108) sts rem. Work as est without further shaping until piece measures 14½ (16½) in / 37 (42) cm.

Dec inside edge st at each side every 4th row a total of 7 times and then on every other row a total of 15 times.
At the same time, after the 5th dec, dec 1 st on each side of the pattern on RS 5 times. When piece measures 27½ (29½) in / 70 (75) cm, BO 2 (2) sts at each side = 38 (50) sts rem for the neck.

Work the neckband following Chart 2. BO when band measures 2½ in / 6 cm.

BACK (St st)

CO 130 (150) sts. Work back and forth in pattern following chart 2 until piece measures 2½ in / 6 cm. On the last WS row, dec 28 (40) sts evenly spaced across = 102 (110) sts rem. On the next RS row, dec 1 st at each side inside each edge st as well as 1 st inside the outermost 12 sts at each side = 4 sts decreased. Work 4 rows and then rep the dec row once more = 94 (102) sts rem. Work as est without further shaping until piece measures 14½ (16½) in / 37 (42) cm. Dec inside edge st at each side every 4th row a total of 7 times and then on every other row a total of 14 (14) times.

At the same time, after the 5th dec, dec 1 st inside the outermost 12 sts at each side on RS 5 times. When piece measures 27½ (29½) in / 70 (75) cm, BO 2 (0) sts at each side = 38 (50) sts rem for the neck.

Work the neckband following chart 2. BO when band measures 2½ in / 6 cm.

FINISHING

Seam the sides, leaving an opening for the arms 6¼ in / 16 cm long, approx. 9½ in / 24 cm up from cast-on edge.

Chart 1

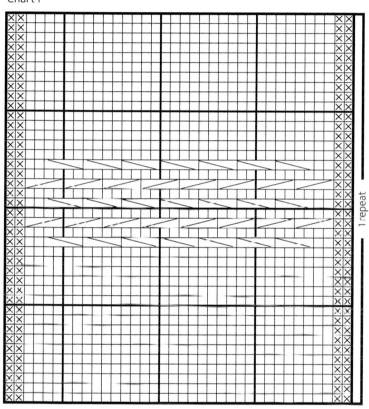

1 repeat

Chart 2

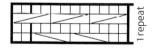

1 repeat

NOTE: On the 1st row, k2, (C4F) until 2 sts rem and end with k2.

☐   Knit on RS, purl on WS

☒   Purl on RS, knit on WS

▱   Sl 2 sts to cn and hold in front of work, k2, k2 from cn

▱   Sl 2 sts to cn and hold in back of work, k2, k2 from cn

INCA PATTERN PONCHO

Design: Turid Stapnes

SIZES
6-8 (10-12) years; S/M (L/XL)

FINISHED MEASUREMENTS
TOTAL LENGTH: 23¾ (25½, 27½, 29½) in / 60 (65, 70, 75) cm

Circumference, lower edge: 83 (87¾, 92, 96¾) in / 211 (223, 234, 246) cm

MATERIALS
YARN: CYCA #5 (bulky) Hobbygarn from Viking of Norway (100% wool; 82 yd/75 m / 50 g)

YARN AMOUNTS:

350 (400, 450, 450) g Light Gray 913 OR Beige 907

200 (250, 250, 300) g White 900

+ 50 g of MC for hood

NEEDLES: U.S. sizes 9 and 10 / 5.5 and 6 mm, circulars

GAUGE: 14 sts in St st on larger needles = 4 in / 10 cm. Adjust needle sizes to obtain correct gauge if necessary.

This is the only pattern in the book that also comes in children's sizes, but it won't be difficult to adapt the other designs for smaller sizes if you have some experience at adjusting patterns. You can decide if you want a high turtleneck or a hood on this poncho, which is worked in the round.

PONCHO

With White and larger needles, CO 296 (312, 328, 344) sts. Join, being careful not to twist cast-on row. Pm for beg of rnd and a different color/style of markers to divide the piece into four sections with 74 (78, 82, 86) sts between each marker. One marker is at center front, one at right side, one at center back, and the last one on the left side. Work around in pattern following Chart 1.

Begin decreasing at center front and center back as indicated by arrows. The arrow on the chart indicates the first rnd of decreases: Work until 2 sts before the marker, ssk, slm, k2tog. Decrease the same way at center back.

Decrease the same way on every other rnd. After completing charted rows, continue in St st with Light Gray Beige. After 38 (40, 42, 44) decrease rnds, begin decreasing at the sides also, *on every 4ᵗʰ rnd*, as at front and back 4 (4, 5, 5) times. Now dec every other rnd until 60 (60, 64, 64) sts rem.

TURTLENECK
Change to smaller circular and work around in k1, p1 ribbing for about 4¾ (5½, 6¼, 6¼) in / 12 (14, 16, 16) cm. BO in ribbing.

HOOD
Change to smaller circular and work in k1, p1 ribbing for about ¾ in / 2 cm. Change back to larger circular. Place the 10 (10, 12, 12) center front sts on a holder and then work back and forth in St st. Pm at the center back and inc 1 st on each side of marker every 4ᵗʰ rnd 8 (8, 9, 10) times. Continue until hood measures approx. 9¾ (10¼, 10¾, 11) in / 25 (26, 27, 28) cm (as measured from ribbing). Divide the stitches in half, turn piece so WS is facing out, and join the two sets of sts with three-needle bind-off.

EDGING AROUND HOOD
Slip sts from holder to smaller circular and, with Light Gray (Beige), pick up and knit about 74 (76, 78, 80) sts around the hood = 84 (86, 90, 92) sts total. Work in pattern following Chart 2. BO.

FRINGE
With White, tie a fringe of carpet knots in every eyelet at the lower edge of the poncho. Each fringe should be doubled yarn about 4 in / 10 cm long when finished.

Chart 1

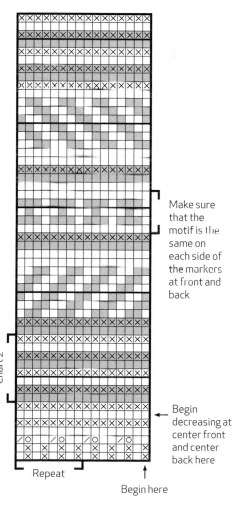

Make sure
that the
motif is the
same on
each side of
the markers
at front and
back

Chart 2

Begin
decreasing at
center front
and center
back here

Repeat

Begin here

☐ White knit
☒ White purl
▨ Gray (Beige) knit
▧ Gray (Beige) purl
⊙ Yarnover
⍁ K2tog

FUR TURTLENECK PONCHO

Design: Denise Samson

SIZES
S (M, L, XL, XXL)

FINISHED MEASUREMENTS
TOTAL LENGTH: 23¼ (25¼, 27½, 30, 32¼) in / 59 (64, 70, 76, 82) cm
CIRCUMFERENCE, LOWER EDGE: 36¼ (38½, 41¼, 43¼, 46) in / 92 (98, 105, 110, 117) cm

MATERIALS
YARN: CYCA #6 (super bulky) Fur from Du Store Alpakka (59% baby alpaca, 41% extra fine Merino wool; 66 yd/60 m / 50 g)
YARN AMOUNTS:
550 (550, 600, 700, 800) g Beige 203
NEEDLES: U.S. sizes 10½ and 11 / 7 and 8 mm, circulars
GAUGE: 11 sts in St st on larger needles = 4 in / 10 cm.
Adjust needle sizes to obtain correct gauge if necessary.

Now you can wear fur with a clear conscience! It's wonderful to have this very soft fur yarn embracing you, and the wrong side looks just as good as the right side. This poncho is worked back and forth in two matching pieces, from the top down. The matching boot toppers will really warm your ankles.

Increases: Increase 1 st at each side of the center stitch with M1—pick up the strand between two stitches and knit into the back of it.

Edge Stitches: Knit the first and last stitch of every row as an edge stitch.

FRONT
Begin at the neck. With smaller circular, CO 29 sts (all sizes). Work back and forth in ribbing as follows: K1 (edge st), (k3, p3) until 4 sts rem and end with k3, k1 edge st). Continue in ribbing as est until piece measures 10¼ in / 26 cm. Change to larger circular and knit 1 row, increasing 10 sts

evenly spaced across = 39 sts. Pm on center st and continue in St st. At the same time, begin increasing 1 st at each side of the center st (see Increases above) on every other row until there are 115 (123, 131, 139, 147) sts. End by knitting 2 rows garter st, increasing as before on the RS row. BO but, to avoid the tip rolling up, knit 2 sts in the st at each side of the center st *at the same time* as you BO. The piece should measure approx. 23¼ (25¼, 27½, 30, 32¼) in / 59 (64, 70, 76, 82) cm at center front measured from the ribbing down.

BACK
With smaller needle, CO 29 sts. Work ribbing as: K1 (edge st), (p3, k3) until 4 sts rem and end with k3, k1 (edge st). Continue as for the front.

FINISHING
Place the pieces with RS matching RS and graft at the sides inside 1 edge st. Seam the top 6¼ in / 16 cm of the neck on the opposite side so that the seam hides where the neck is folded down to the RS.

BOOT TOPPERS

Design: Denise Samson

SIZE
One size

MATERIALS
YARN: CYCA #6 (super bulky) Fur from Du Store Alpakka (59% baby alpaca, 41% extra fine Merino wool; 66 yd/60 m / 50 g)
AND CYCA #4 (worsted) Alpakka/Ull from Sandnes Garn (65% alpaca, 35% wool; 109 yd/100 m / 50 g)
YARN AMOUNTS:
50 g each Fur, Beige 203 and Alpakka/Ull, Beige 2650
NEEDLES: U.S. sizes 8 and 11 / 5 and 8 mm

_____

With smaller needles and Alpakka/Ull, CO 52 sts. Work back and forth in k2, p2 ribbing for 4 in / 10 cm. Cut Alpakka/Ull. Change to larger needles and Fur. K2tog across = 26 sts rem. Knit in garter st until piece measures 8 in / 20 cm from cast-on edge. BO. Using the matching yarns, seam the ribbing and then the fur edging.

MULTI-PURPOSE PONCHO

Design: Hrönn Jónsdóttir

SIZES
XS/S (M/L, XL/XXL)

FINISHED MEASUREMENTS
CIRCUMFERENCE: approx. 86½ (94½, 102¼) in / 220 (240, 260) cm
TOTAL LENGTH, SHOULDER TO LOWER EDGE: approx. 15½ (16½, 19) in / 39 (42, 48) cm

MATERIALS
YARN: CYCA #5 (bulky) Hexa from Du Store Alpakka (100% Merino wool; 109 yd/100 m / 50 g)
YARN AMOUNTS:
800 (850, 950) g Mold 934
NOTIONS: 14 buttons - K360484 from Hjelmtvedt)
NEEDLES: U.S. sizes 10½ / 7 mm, circular; cable needle
CROCHET HOOK: U.S. size J-10 / 6 mm
GAUGE: 16 sts in pattern = 4 in / 10 cm.
Adjust needle size to obtain correct gauge if necessary.

This delightful poncho can be styled multiple ways. By changing how it's buttoned, you can create a completely new garment. The poncho is worked back and forth.

FRONT
CO 62 (67, 77) sts and work in pattern following the chart until the piece measures 86½ (94½, 102¼) in / 220 (240, 260) cm
NOTE: Adjust the length so that you end up at the same place in the cable pattern as at cast-row. BO.

BACK
Work as for Front.

CROCHETED EDGING
Crochet an edging all around as follows: Begin with 1 sl st at a corner on the front or back. Work (ch 3, skip about ⅝ in / 1.5 cm, 1 sl st in edge) all around except at the corners where you work (1 sl st + ch 2 + 1 sl st) into the same st.

FINISHING
Mark off 9¾ (11, 12¼) in / 25 (28, 31) cm centered on one long side of the back. Sew a button on each side of the marker and another 6 buttons on each side evenly spaced along the edge facing the cast-on/bound-off edge, a total of 14 buttons. Instead of buttonholes, make crocheted ch loops along the front and back edges so the pieces can be buttoned in several different ways or each piece can be used as a scarf.

Chart

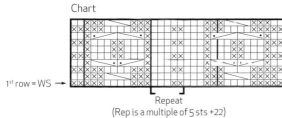

1st row = WS →

Repeat
(Rep is a multiple of 5 sts +22)

☐ Knit on RS, purl on WS

☒ Purl on RS, knit on WS

Sl 2 sts to cn and hold in front of work k2, k2 from cn

Sl 2 knit sts to cn and hold in front of work, p2, k2 from cn

Sl 2 purl sts to cn and hold in back of work, k2, p2 from cn

PONCHO WITH DIAMOND CABLES

Design: Turid Stapnes

SIZE
One size

FINISHED MEASUREMENTS
SHOULDER WIDTH: 35½ in / 90 cm
TOTAL LENGTH AT CENTER FRONT: 29½ in / 75 cm
CIRCUMFERENCE AT LOWER EDGE: 97 in / 246 cm

MATERIALS
YARN: CYCA #5 (bulky) Alpaca Maya from Viking of Norway (82% alpaca, 13% Merino wool, 5% polyamide; 175 yd/160 m / 50 g)
YARN AMOUNTS:
200 g Gray 715
NEEDLES: U.S. sizes 10 and 10½ / 6 and 7 mm, 24 in / 60 cm circular in smaller and varying lengths of circulars in larger (change as necessary to accommodate sts)
GAUGE: 12 sts in St st on larger needles = 4 in / 10 cm.
Adjust needle sizes to obtain correct gauge if necessary.

———————

An elegant poncho with large diamond cables worked in a soft alpaca yarn. The poncho is worked in the round on large needles. The ribbed neckband makes the poncho nice and cozy.

PONCHO

With larger circular, CO 296 sts. Join, being careful not to twist cast-on row. Pm for beg of rnd and a different color/style of markers to divide the piece into four sections with 74 sts between each marker. One marker is at center back, one at the left side, one at center front, and the last at the right side.

The rnd begins 2 sts before the marker at center back. Work 4 sts in St st, 144 sts following chart, 4 sts St st (= center front) 144 sts in charted pattern. Continue around as est. When the piece measures about ¾ in / 2 cm, begin decreasing at center front and center back as follows: work until 3 sts before the marker, k2tog, k1, slm, k1, ssk. Repeat the decreases at the center back marker. Decrease the same way on every other rnd until 108 sts rem. Now begin *also* decreasing at the sides (dec 1 st on each side of each side marker) on every other rnd. When 88 sts rem, change to smaller circular and work in k1, p1 ribbing for about 4 in / 10 cm. BO in ribbing. Weave in all ends neatly on WS.

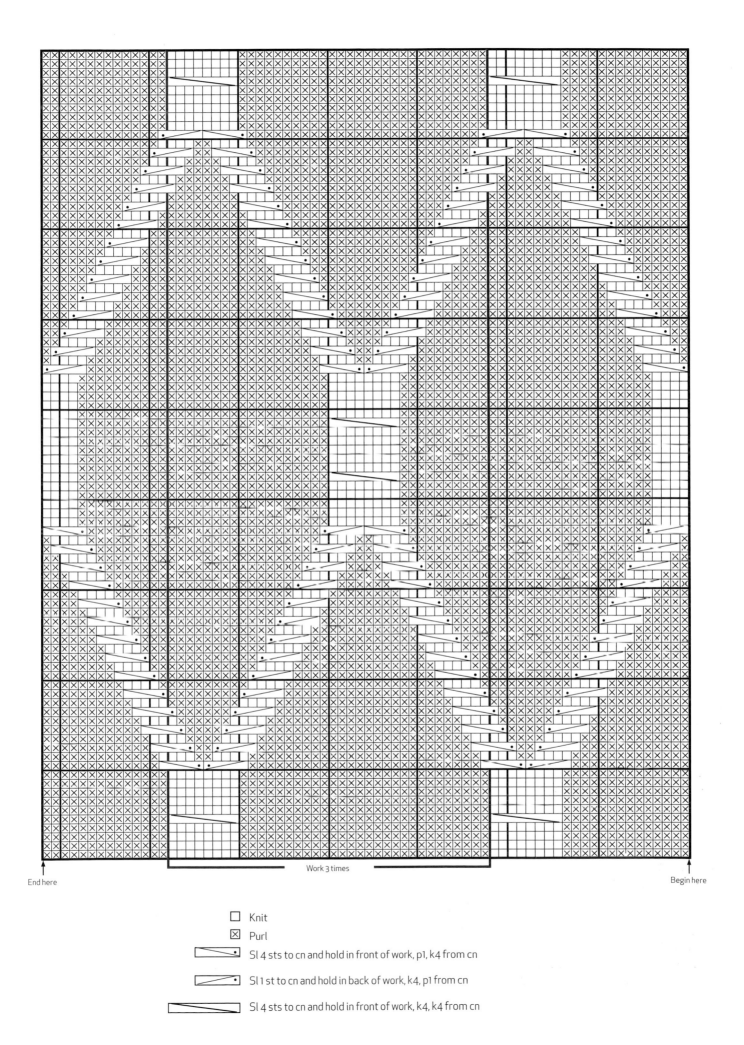

Work 3 times

End here

Begin here

☐ Knit

☒ Purl

Sl 4 sts to cn and hold in front of work, p1, k4 from cn

Sl 1 st to cn and hold in back of work, k4, p1 from cn

Sl 4 sts to cn and hold in front of work, k4, k4 from cn

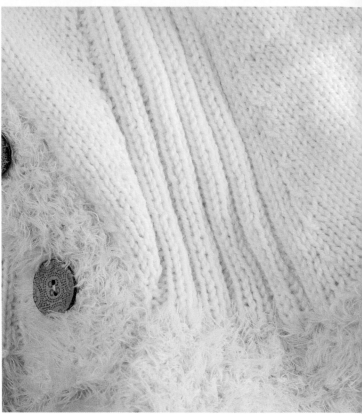

PONCHO WITH FURRY TRIM

Design: Denise Samson

SIZE
One size

FINISHED MEASUREMENTS
CIRCUMFERENCE, LOWER EDGE: 69¼ in / 176 cm
TOTAL LENGTH: 27½ in / 70 cm
COWL: 22¾ x 6¼ in / 58 x 16 cm

MATERIALS
YARN: CYCA #4 (worsted/afghan/Aran) Cotinga from Dale Garn (70% Merino wool, 30% alpaca; 87 yd/80 m / 50 g)
AND CYCA #6 (super bulky) Fur from Du Store Alpakka (59% baby alpaca, 41% extra fine Merino wool; 66 yd/60 m / 50 g)
YARN AMOUNTS:
600 g Cotinga, Natural White 0020
300 g Fur, Natural White 202
NOTIONS: 8 large wood buttons

NEEDLES: U.S. sizes 8 and 11 / 5 and 8 mm, 16 and 32 in / 40 and 80 cm circulars and set of 5 dpn
GAUGE:
FUR: 10 sts in St st on larger needles = 4 in / 10 cm.
COTINGA: 18 sts in St st on smaller needles = 4 in / 10 cm.
Adjust needle sizes to obtain correct gauge if necessary.

A large square poncho with ribbing moving on the bias up to the neck. The wonderful furry edging is the height of winter elegance. The poncho is worked back and forth in two matching pieces that are sewn together in finishing. The buttons at the side are purely decorative.

FRONT
With larger circular and Fur, CO 104 sts. Knit 8 rows in garter st (the 1st row = WS). Change to smaller circular. On next row, WS, knit across, increasing as follows: (K5, M1) 20 times, end with k4 = 124 sts. Change to Cotinga yarn.

Now continue as follows:

Row 1: Work 20 sts in k2, p2 ribbing, 84 sts St st, 20 sts in p2, k2 ribbing.

Row 2: Work knit over knit and purl over purl.

Row 3: K2, M1, (p2, k2) 5 times, k2tog, 76 sts St st, ssk, (k2, p2) 5 times, M1, p2.

Rows 4–6: Work knit over knit and purl over purl.

Row 7: K3, M1, (p2, k2) 5 times, k2tog, 74 St sts, ssk, (k2, p2) 5 times, M1, p3.

Row 8: Work knit over knit and purl over purl.

Rep Rows 5-8 with 1 st more before each increase and 2 sts less before each decrease on the front until piece measures 27½ in / 70 cm. BO in pattern.

Make the back the same way.

EDGES ON EACH SIDE

With larger circular and Fur, pick up and knit 82 sts along the left side of the front. Knit 10 rows. Do the same on the opposite side as well as on both sides of the back.

FINISHING

Seam the shoulders up to the ribbing on each side. Arrange the sections so that one furry edge overlaps the other. Measure out 15¾ in / 40 cm from the cast-on edge and place a pin through both pieces. Place 4 markers evenly spaced with the bottom one 2 in / 5 cm from the cast-on edge, the top one 1¼ in / 3 cm from the pin, and the last two evenly spaced between the top and bottom mark-

ers. Sew on 4 buttons as marked. The buttons are decorative only. Finally, with one strand of Fur, sew the 15¾ in / 40 cm long overlap on each side with whip stitch. Overlap and stitch the opposite side the same way.

COWL

With Fur and the short larger circular, CO 66 sts. Join, being careful not to twist cast-on row; pm for beg of rnd. Work 6 rnds in garter st (alternate knit and purl rnds) and then continue in St st until piece measures 5¼ in / 13 cm. End with 6 rnds garter st. BO loosely.

DETACHED CUFFS

With smaller dpn and Cotinga, CO 44 sts; divide sts onto dpn and join. Work around in k2 p2 ribbing for 4 in / 10 cm. Change to larger dpn and Fur. On the first rnd with Fur, k2tog over each of the purl ribs = 33 sts rem. Continue in St st until piece measures 4 in / 10 cm. BO. Fold the Fur edge over the ribbing.

KNITTING TIPS

If you want a tighter Fur edge, work k2tog over both the knit and purl ribs when you change to Fur = 22 sts rem.

GLITTERY CROCHETED SHAWL

Design: Denise Samson

SIZE
One size

FINISHED MEASUREMENTS
Approx. 25¼ x 55 in / 64 x 140 cm

MATERIALS
YARN: CYCA #1 (fingering) Fin from Du Store Alpakka
(50% alpaca, 50% silk; 180 yd/165 m / 50 g)
AND Güterman Sulky Glitter Thread (foil laminated with polyester)
YARN AMOUNTS:
500 g Fin, Red 226
1 spool Sulky Glitter thread, Silver 6001
NOTIONS: 6 silver buttons
CROCHET HOOK: U.S. size E-4 / 3.5 mm

_____

This shawl can be worn several different ways: as a regular shawl, as a sweater that you button at the sides to make sleeves, or as a bolero buttoned at the front. If you want to add a little glam, use glitter thread as suggested—but you can omit it if you prefer.

The pattern is a multiple of 8 sts + 2 (plus 4 ch on the foundation chain).

SHAWL
Ch 158.

Row 1: In the 7th ch from hook, work (1 dc, ch 2, 1 dc), *skip 3 ch, work (2 dc, ch 1, 2 dc) in next ch, skip 3 ch, (1 dc, ch 2, 1 dc) in next ch*. Rep * to * to the last 7 ch, skip 3 ch, (2 dc, ch 1, 2 dc) in next ch, skip 2 ch, 1 dc in last ch; turn.
Row 2: Ch 3, skip first dc, *(1 dc, ch 2, 1 dc) in ch loop, skip 3 dc, (2 dc, ch 1, 2 dc) in next ch loop, skip 3 dc*. Rep * to * and end with 1 dc in last st; turn. Rep Row 2 but end with 1 dc in the 3rd ch; turn. Work in pattern until piece measures 55 in / 140 cm or desired length.

EDGING
Do not cut yarn but work a single crochet edging: Work 2 sc in each ch loop and 4 sc in each corner. Join with 1 sl st to 1st sc; cut yarn and bring end through last loop. Weave in all ends neatly on WS.

FINISHING
Sew 3 buttons on each side (the long side) with 5¼ in / 13 cm between each button. Use the holes in the pattern for "natural" buttonholes.

YARN SOURCES

DU STORE ALPAKKA
www.dustorealpakka.com

DALE GARN
www.dalegarnnorthamerica.com

ARTYARNS (for Artyarns Ensemble Glitter)
www.artyarns.com

DROPS
www.garnstudio.com

MANOS DEL URUGUAY
U.S.: www.fairmountfibers.com
Canada: www.estelleyarns.com/manos-del-uruguay.php
U.K and Europe: www.artesanoyarns.co.uk

SANDNES GARN
www.sandnesgarn.com

If you are unable to obtain any of the yarn used in this book, it can be replaced with a yarn of a similar weight and composition. Please note, however, the finished projects may vary slightly from those shown, depending on the yarn used. Try www.yarnsub.com for suggestions.

For more information on selecting or substituting yarn, contact your local yarn shop or an online store; they are familiar with all types of yarns and would be happy to help you. Additionally, the online knitting community at Ravelry.com has forums where you can post questions about specific yarns. Yarns come and go so quickly these days and there are so many beautiful yarns available.